THE BUSHIDO CODE

Words of Wisdom from
Japan's Greatest Samurai

TADASHI KAMIKO

Translated with an Introduction by
William Scott Wilson

TUTTLE Publishing
Tokyo | Rutland, Vermont | Singapore

Contents

The Arts of Peace and
the Arts of War
by William Scott Wilson

DURING ONE OF THE MANY battles that took place at the turn of the seventeenth century, the warlord and general, Furuta Oribe (1544–1615), was running through a bamboo grove that was being showered by a fusillade of bullets, when he suddenly looked down and saw a small piece of bamboo. Struck by its size and shape, he stopped for a few moments and carved an elegant *chashaku*—a teaspoon used in the tea ceremony—and then charged on. Oribe was a noted warrior—he had first joined the forces of Oda Nobunaga, the most powerful general of the era, and after that man's death, those of his successor, Toyotomi Hideyoshi, fighting both in Japan and in Hideyoshi's invasions of Korea in the 1590s. But he was also a tea master and a potter, creating teahouses, landscaped gardens and tea-ceremony utensils. During the latter part of his life, Oribe revolutionized the ambiance of the tea ceremony, and was recognized as a warrior and an arbiter of taste, yet in 1615, he was accused of conspiracy against the central government, was ordered to commit ritual suicide, and did so without a word of protest.

🔥   🔥   🔥

The Warring States period (1467–1615; also known as the Sengoku period) was perhaps the most violent and chaotic era in Japanese history. Clan fought against clan, subordinates overthrew their overlords, factions changed incessantly, and the resulting civil war all but destroyed the ancient capital of Kyoto. Leaders of the warrior houses learned new levels of opportunism and ruthlessness, and the common assessment of their characters by later writers is one of general moral decline.

Yet no less an historian than George Sansom found this to be the most interesting period of Japan's development; and dedicated an entire volume of his three-part *History of Japan* to this era. And, it is often noted that, it was exactly in this climate of chaotic change and strife that some of Japan's finest cultural achievements—Noh drama, tea ceremony, Zen temple gardening and linked verse, to name a few—either found their beginnings or their highest points.

It should also be noted that, despite the judgment of "moral decline" on the part of the leaders of the warrior clans, some of their finest, most philosophically and psychologically uplifting, and interesting sayings, precepts and anecdotes found expression during this time. These warriors were practical men who had to deal with the very grim conditions of survival, and those without insight to their environments and the personalities of their peers would not last long. At the same time, such men were not simply rough uneducated fighters, but often, like Furuta Oribe, personified the Far Eastern ideal of balancing cultural awareness and artistic expertise with high martial abilities. Indeed, the cultural (文) and the martial (武) were understood by them to be mutually supportive, like the two wings of a bird. Or, as the warlord Kuroda Nagamasa (1568–1623) noted,

> The arts of peace and the arts of war are like the two
> wheels of a cart which, lacking one, will have difficulty
> in standing.

This ideal was an ancient one, and the balance of these two qualities appeared in the Chinese lexicon in the form of the single character 斌 as early as the first century BC. In Japanese, it can be pronounced either *hin* or *uruwashii*, and by extension can mean beautiful, elegant or harmonious—a balance between the exterior pattern (文) and interior essence or substance (武). Again, we think of Furuta Oribe and the tea ceremony, but other warlords and warriors were experts in lacquerware, painting, flower arranging, poetry and calligraphy, and we find a sense of this quality of personal balance in the writings of many of the warriors quoted in this volume. Consequently, their sayings, precepts—even those focused on the survival of the clan—and the anecdotes about them are informed by a broad spectrum of interests, many of which may apply to those of us living in the twenty-first century. The courage and ambition to face our daily affairs, the insights necessary for dealing with both compatriots and opponents, the value of art and literature and even the problems of why and how to save money are intimately part and parcel of our own modern interests. It was, however, the intensity of their concerns that sharpened and honed their recorded language to its most distilled and succinct quality.

★　　★　　★

This book is a translation of the Japanese work *Sengoku busho goroku* (戦国武将の語録, lit. "Recorded sayings of the generals of the Warring States period"). I am deeply indebted to the scholar Tadashi Kamiko who compiled and edited the original Japanese work and added insightful commentary. A number of Kamiko's works line my library, including those on *Hagakure*, *Saikontan* and Sun Tzu.

All footnotes in this book are those of the translator.

The Values of Bushido
by William Scott Wilson

THE CONCEPT OF BUSHIDO 武士道, the Way of the Warrior, seems to have germinated during the Nara period (710–794), with the consolidation of the various clans centered around the area of Yamato, and formulated into a distinct idea during the Kamakura period (1185–1333) at the establishment of the shogunate. The term *Bushido* perhaps first appeared in writing in the *Koyo gunkan*, a work completed in 1616 describing the military exploits of the Takeda clan: "There is not the least bit of [personal] gain to be had in the Way of the Warrior" 武士道の益に立 事聊かもなし (*Bushido no yaku ni tatsu koto isasaka mo nashi*). It is also famously quoted in the book *Hagakure*, (c. 1716): "The Way of the Warrior is found in death" 武士道といふは死事と 見付たり (*Bushido to iu wa shinu koto to mitsuketari*).

But what does *bushi* mean? The word is an ancient one, found at its earliest in the Chinese classic historical text, *Records of the Grand Historian*, finished around 100 BC. Deconstructing the word *bu* 武, we find that it is made up of two characters: 止, "to stop, and an abbreviation of 弋, "halberd" or "tasseled spear." There is no agreement on whether this would mean "to stop with a spear" or the more pacifist "to stop the spear," but two ancient Chinese references indicate the latter. The dictionary, the *Shuowen jiezi* (c. 181 A.D.) has the following definition: "*Bu* consists of subduing the weapon, and therefore stopping the spear." The historical document, the *Tso Chuan* (c. 400 BC) says "*Bu* prohibits violence and subdues weapons [. . .] It puts the people at peace."

Shi 士, however, archaically seems to have represented a battle ax and implied the rank of a warrior, complimenting *bu*. In the

Analects of Confucius, the sage Confucius remarks, "A *shi* is some-one who conducts himself with an awareness of shame. When sent out in the four directions, he brings no shame upon his lord [. . .] He will always stand by his words, and his actions and be-havior will always bear fruit." (*Analects*, 7:20) And later, "He is polite, effective and in accord with others." (*Analects*, 7:14) In Ja-pan, this *shi* came to be understood as a learned or cultured man, and the word *bushi* an educated warrior; and the ideal was for any warrior to be cultured. Thus *Bushido* became the Way (道 , etymologically "an intelligent way of moving") of the Warrior.

The warrior clans ruled Japan for roughly seven hundred years, from 1160 to 1868. During that time, the predominant ideology would have been Bushido or some nascent pattern of warrior thought. And this would not have been limited to the warriors themselves, but would necessarily have percolated downward through the various classes all the way to the farmers in the fields, who were well aware of their overlords. But there were numer-ous clans throughout Japan and, just as dialects developed in the different provinces, so did the interpretations of Bushido vary from place to place, depending on the history of the clan and the personality or outlook of the different warlords.

Kuroda Nagamasa, for example, was enfeoffed in the prov-ince of Chikuzen and was baptized as a Christian. He emphasized the practice of love and humanity in the administration of the fief, and lay heavy importance on the study of literature. The lord of nearby Kumamoto Castle, Kato Kiyomasa, on the other hand, declared that a warrior's "intentions should be to grasp the long and short swords and to die." He stated further that "read-ing Chinese poetry, linked verse and classical Japanese poetry is forbidden." Another interesting example is the extreme caution taken by the shogun Tokugawa Ieyasu, who told his retainers that "Hiking your robe up above your buttocks when crossing a river that only comes up to your knees, may seem a little too cautious, but you won't have the problem of getting wet." Compare this to Yamamoto Tsunetomo, a samurai of the Nabeshima clan, who wrote, "The Way of the Warrior is found in death. When it comes to a matter of either/or, there is only the quick choice of death. It is not particularly difficult; be determined and advance." One other example might be the advice of Hojo Shigetoki, the military governor of the province of Suruga: "One should worship the gods and Buddhas morning and night, and maintain a heart of faith. The gods grant power to a man according to his respect for them, and he maintains his fate according to their blessings." Compare this with the statement of Miyamoto Musashi, Japan's most famous swordsman. "Respect the gods and Buddhas, but do not depend on them."

Bushido therefore was not one precise and exact code, but was organic and vital. Nevertheless, over the centuries, certain values developed that were estimated as central to a warrior's way of life.

忠 Loyalty. The first and foremost value: primarily to one's lord, then to family and finally to friends and fellow samurai.

孝 Filial piety. This includes not only faithfulness to one's own immediate family, but to the long line of ancestors who labored hard so that the individual could exist.

勇 Courage. Not just to face the enemy in battle, but also that needed to reprimand one's lord when necessary, regardless of the personal consequences.

名誉 Honor or prestige. Not only to one's self, but to one's family, lord and clan. But a samurai must be judicious.

Military commander Takeda Shingen warned, "a man wants fame to the extent that he does not get results."

禮義 Propriety. Manners or decorum. This quality of behavior is to be maintained at all times, with one's lord, one's family and one's companions. Even when merrymaking, the warrior should maintain proper demeanor. Otherwise his honor and reputation may be at stake.

信義 Faithfulness. Literally, standing by one's words.

廉潔 Uprightness and honesty. A samurai must never be questioned or doubted as to his real intents. Both his lord and his companions must have full confidence in his motivations and truthfulness.

質素 Simplicity, frugality and modesty. These apply to personal apparel, domicile, eating habits and every-day behavior. Modesty, combined with courage, was exemplified in the Chinese classic text, *Records of the Grand Historian*: "Meng Chih-fan was not boastful. In retreat, he took up the rear position. As he was about to enter the gate, he whipped his horse and said, 'It's not that I dared to be last, the horse just wouldn't go.'"

慈愛 Benevolence. A true warrior will never be arrogant, and will always look with sympathy on those less fortunate than he. This quality should be manifested in his actions as well as his mental attitude.

誠 Sincerity. The Chinese character means "when words become reality." This was a main tenet of Bushido, and the bedrock upon which all the other qualities had their foundation. In the Confucian text *Doctrine of the Mean*, it states, "Sincerity is the Way of Heaven. Putting sincerity into practice is the Way of Man. Sincerity hits the target without effort, and grasps [what is correct] without thought [. . .] Sincerity is the beginning and end of all things." Sincerity was the quality with which one walked through life and fought on the battlefield.

The values of Bushido are not historical curiosities unrelated to present times, but are securely absorbed in the cultural consciousness of the Japanese today. Turn on children's TV cartoons and, along with the fantastic robots and exciting adventures of wayward kids, are embedded the lessons of courage, honesty and selflessness; Japanese workers are famous for their loyalty to their workplaces; respect for others extends to the homeless and shabbily dressed; and decorum is emphasized at every level of society.

The title of this book in its original Japanese version is *Sengoku busho goroku* (戦国武将の語録, lit. "Recorded sayings of the generals of the Warring States period"). It is an anthology of the sayings, precepts and anecdotes relating to the most famous of the warrior leaders of that era. Readers of Japanese history and culture may be familiar with some of these personalities—Takeda Shingen, Oda Nobunaga, Tokugawa Ieyasu and Kato Kiyomasa, for example. But others like Hosokawa Yusai, Baba Nobufusa and Gamo Ujisato, although every bit as interesting, will be relatively unknown; and many of their precepts contained in this book have become a sort of common knowledge to the modern Japanese, whether the original quote can be immediately recalled or not, and thus run through some of the currents of Japanese thinking even today. When we Westerners relate the Bushido code only to the samurai of old, we have perhaps, in the words of the warlord Nabeshima Naoshige, only seen the flower and not the fruit.

THE WARRIORS

Ota Dokan
(1432–1486)

DOKAN WAS THE FAMOUS general who built Edo Castle, which would become the seat of power for Tokugawa Ieyasu, the first shogun of the Edo period, more than a hundred years later. For this reason, Dokan is considered by many to be the true founder of Edo (modern-day Tokyo).

As well as Edo Castle, he built the castles at Iwatsuki and Kawagoe. He was a principal retainer of the Uesugi clan, for whom he traveled tirelessly throughout the country. In his later years, he became a Buddhist monk, and devoted himself to traditional Japanese poetry. In 1486, he was slandered by rivals and, as a result, assassinated by the order of his lord, Uesugi Sadamasa.

                     ▲   ▲   ▲

> If you are not impatient,
>> you will not be drenched:
> The traveler's hasty footprints,
>> on the muddy path through the fields,
>> after the rain.

This was Dokan's response, in traditional poetic form, when Hosokawa Katsumoto, a deputy to the shogun, asked him the meaning of the phrase, "A hot temper will make no great accomplishments." At the heart of the poem is the notion that one will accomplish one's aim not by acting unreasonably, but by going with the flow of things.

Once, seven of Dokan's retainers committed a crime, and were given a sentence of death. The retainers, however, ensconced themselves in a house, and would not come out. Dokan beckoned one of his most able men, and whispered something in his ear. The man then went over to the house, and yelled loudly enough so that all inside could hear:

"Listen up, all you samurai who have this house surrounded. Lord Dokan has said that he is going to spare one of the seven men inside, so do not cut them down indiscriminately!" The men in the house were taken aback, each thinking that it would be he himself who was to be pardoned. At first, one of them was cut down, but the other six offered no resistance. In this way, all seven were eventually executed.

At another time, Dokan visited the capital, and was invited to a banquet at the mansion of the shogun. Before he was to attend, however, someone pulled him aside and informed him, "The shogun often keeps a pet monkey at his side. This animal will attack people it's unfamiliar with, so please be careful." Dokan thereupon gave the shogun's monkey keeper some gold, secretly borrowed the monkey, and tied it up in his garden. He then dressed himself in his formal clothing, and approached the beast. When the monkey attacked him, he struck it with his whip, and repeated this until the monkey treated him with fear and respect. On the day of the banquet, the shogun thought he would put Dokan to a test, and purposefully brought the monkey to his guest's side. At the sight of Dokan, the monkey furtively curled up its tail and scampered away. With an innocent face, Dokan then received the shogun's hospitality.

Hojo Soun
(1432–1519)

SOUN WAS A GENERAL and vassal of the Imagawa clan, which ruled the area of Suruga. He eventually supplanted that clan, making the castle at Odawara his own. There, he created one of the first great castle towns of the period, lessening the taxes on the peasants, and attracting warriors from other provinces. He was known as an able administrator, a sympathetic overlord, but also as a perspicacious general. He eventually shaved his head, and became a Buddhist priest. The painting of him housed at the Soun temple in the town of Hakone Yumoto is said to depict his stubborn will and sharp expressive eyes. He died at the great age of eighty-eight, a year after successfully besieging a rival's castle.

After Soun became a priest, he wrote a list of precepts known as *The Twenty-one Articles*, as a summary of admonitions and advice for the later retainers of the Hojo clan, and they are indicative of his attention to the minute details and rhythm of daily life.

- Believe in the gods and Buddhas.
- Arise early in the morning.
- You should be asleep before eight o'clock in the evening. Rise at four in the morning, wash yourself and pray, arrange your proper attire, instruct your wife, children and retainers of the day's chores, and report to your station before six in the morning.
- Before washing your face and hands, inspect the toilet areas, the stables, the garden and the area outside of the gate. Give

commands to the appropriate people to sweep the places that need to be cleaned, and only then quickly wash yourself.

- Prayer is the proper action of your station.
- You should not envy the swords and clothing of others. Just prepare yourself so that such things will not be unsightly.
- It goes without saying that you should arrange your hair early in the morning if you are going out to your work, but this should be done even if you are thinking of staying at home.
- When you arrive for your duties, you should simply appear casually before your lord.
- If you have been spoken to by your lord, first respond readily even if you are waiting upon him at some distance. Then come forward quickly on your knees, and receive his commands respectfully.
- You should not be close by when someone is passing along information to your lord. You should withdraw to the side.
- A saying has it that when you associate with a number of people, you should not stir up strife. Regardless of the event, you should defer to others.
- Whenever you have even a little spare time, you should take out a book or some written material you have placed in your robe, and read it out of the sight of others.
- When you are passing a place where clan elders are in attendance to the lord, you should stoop just a little and make a polite gesture as you go by.
- You should not tell even the smallest lie, regardless of the station of the person to whom you are speaking.
- A person who does not know the Way of Poetry will be poorer for his ignorance. Poetry is something you should study.
- When you are not busy at your duties, you should practice horsemanship. After you have mastered the fundamentals, you should train yourself in the more advanced techniques.
- If you would search out good friends, you will find them among

those with whom you study calligraphy and Learning.[1] If you would avoid bad friends, leave off those who play the games *go* and *shogi*, and musical instruments such as the flute and the shakuhachi.

- When you return to your lodging, you should walk around the stables from front and back, tour the four walls where the dogs may have been digging, and make the proper repairs.
- You should close the gate to your residence tightly by six o'clock in the evening, and open it again only as people need to go in and out.
- Every evening, you yourself should pass through the kitchen and living room checking for fire, and speak strictly on this account.
- It goes without saying that the Way of the Warrior constantly resides in both Learning and the Martial. It is an ancient law that you should have Learning on the left and the Martial on the right, but if you have not prepared this previously, it is not something you can have at hand.

Other words of wisdom from Soun demonstrate his long-range perspective, and an essential part of his character. And indeed, the entire Kanto area fell into the hands of Soun's grandson, Hojo Ujiyasu, who brought the castle town of Odawara to its hitherto most flourishing period.

It is uncertain if a young man who cannot see through the minds of others will be a fool later on. But to imprudently award a fief to such a man, and then to take away his land

---

1. Learning (学 or 学問): less in a scholastic sense than in a good foundation of Confucianism.

after his many mistakes, will cause resentment, not only in the man himself, but in able men in the entire clan.

Gold and silver should be laid in stock for the next three generations. By the third generation, our enemy the Uesugi clan will surely fall, and doubtlessly the entire Kanto area will be within our grasp.

Hojo Ujitsuna
(1487–1541)

UJITSUNA SUCCEEDED HIS FATHER, Hojo Soun, as leader of the Hojo clan, at the age of thirty-three. It was he who captured the castle town of Odawara and made it the base of the clan. At the age of thirty-eight he attacked Edo Castle, then under the control of the Ogiya Uesugi clan. By the time he was forty-nine, he had defeated the Takeda clan in Kai Province, taking the castles of Kawagoe and Matsuyama. It soon appeared that he would have the entire Kanto area in his hands, but he became ill and passed away at the age of fifty-five.

🔱　　🔱　　🔱

Man's life is short. One should never concoct base intentions.

The notion that life is short is not particular to times of upheaval like the one in which Ujitsuna lived. But the response to that notion—the answer to the question of how, really, do we live our lives—changes from age to age. Some three hundred years before Ujitsuna, the reclusive author Kamo no Chomei wrote the following in his collection of essays, the *Hojoki* (An account of my hut):

"The flow of the river is unending, but the water is never the same. The bubbles that float in the backwaters, now appear, now disappear, and there are no examples of their remaining for long [. . .].

This is not unlike the dew on the morning glory. The dew falls and the flower remains. And though we may say that it "remains," it withers in the morning sun."

One hundred years later, the Japanese monk Yoshida Kenko in his *Essays in Idleness*, expressed the transience of life thus:

"This is not a world in which we can live forever. And why would we want to wait around, just to witness our own decrepit features?"

Life is short, so do we act positively and with vigor, or with simple resignation to its limits? These are quite different responses to the very basic question of how we approach the world.

The samurai Yamamoto Tsunetomo (1659–1719) took up the subject in his book, *Hagakure*:

"The life of a human being is truly short. And we should live our lives doing the things we like. In this world that lasts only for the interval of dream, it would be foolish to do only the things we find unpleasant, and to see nothing but bitterness. This is an esoteric truth, and one we do not discuss with young people as they may misunderstand its meaning and do themselves harm. At this juncture, I think it would be appropriate for me to withdraw from the world and spend my days sleeping."

Hojo Ujiyasu
(1515–1571)

WHEN HIS FATHER UJITSUNA died in 1541, Ujiyasu was almost immediately attacked by various rivals in the area. Through a combination of diplomacy and military maneuvering, however, he pacified those would have defeated him, and brought the Hojo stronghold of Odawara to even greater power and prosperity. Ujiyasu was resourceful and practical, ordering his soldiers to wear less armor to allow them more speed in battle, and prohibiting the taking of enemy heads for the same reason. He is said to have had unusual ability in both the administrative and military arts.

✦　　✦　　✦

Do not steal the meritorious deeds of your underlings.

This is advice Ujiyasu gave to his son Ujimasa (1538–1590). Ujiyasu believed that if you were ignorant of the real deeds and circumstances of your underlings, you would not be able to raise their meritorious deeds fairly. This he considered the same as stealing those meritorious deeds. In the same way, in today's workplace, if a superior fails to properly praise his underlings' good works and displays them as his own, he has usurped them.

✦　　✦　　✦

It is normal for a lord to choose his retainers. But there are also times when a retainer will choose his lord. When you

are battling with your neighboring provinces, if you have not shown affection for your retainers or treated the common people well on a daily basis, they may leave, travel to another province, and seek out a brighter lord and a better general there. Thus, showing affection to retainers and treating the common people well is a lord's duty. You must take care of these things yourself, and not delegate them to the elder retainers of the clan.

These words were also directed to Ujimasa, who is said to have come to a sudden deep understanding upon hearing them.

🔥   🔥   🔥

Once, Ujiyasu was eating a meal with Ujimasa, when he suddenly began to shed tears, and lamented, "I can see that the Hojo line is going to end with me!" When Ujimasa and all those in attendance assured him that this could not be true, Ujiyasu continued: "Ujimasa! Look at the way you're eating! You're putting two helpings of sauce on every bowl of rice. People usually eat every day, regardless of their position in life, and should become accustomed to the way of taking a meal. Yet, you still don't understand the proper portion of sauce to rice. What kind of thing is this that one helping is not enough for you, and that you have to add even more? If you are not even aware of what you are doing every morning and night, how will you be able to judge the minds of people who have not yet come before you? If you are not able to understand a man's mind, you will not be able to employ good retainers. If you are unable to employ men of good character, I doubt if you will be able to defend our province."

Mori Motonari
(1497–1571)

MORI MOTONARI BEGAN as the daimyo of Aki, a small fief in what is now Hiroshima Prefecture, and laid the foundation for what would become the Mori clan's dominance of the entire Chugoku (central provinces) area. During his life, he fought over 220 battles, and added ten provinces to his clan's domain. He was not above turning against former allies, and furthered his influence by having two of his sons adopted by other daimyo. When not engaged in battle, he turned to cultural affairs, and was a respected poet.

When Mori Motonari was twelve years old, he went to Ikutsushima Shrine to pray. After, he asked his attendants what they had prayed for. Most of his retinue gave answers they thought would please him; one of them responded, "I prayed that our young lord would be able to make the Chugoku region his own possession."

Motonari looked displeased and said, "Why didn't you pray that I would be able to take all of Japan?"

"First," the man replied, "you take the Chugoku region. Then the rest should follow."

"If you intend to take all of Japan, you will ultimately take the Chugoku region," Motonari retorted. "If you only intend to take the Chugoku region, what will you take then?"

The story illustrates Motonari's belief that you should make yourself great goals.

✦   ✦   ✦

The man whose wisdom excels all others, and who uses his mind to deal with the exigencies of the world, will have no true friends in this world. His only true friends will be the great men of the distant past, and the discriminating men far in the future.

This Motonari once said with a sigh as he leaned against a pillar drinking sake, and looking up to the sky.

✦   ✦   ✦

When a military commander employs men, he must also carefully employ his own mind. Men who are both good and gentle are liable not to offend others, and for this reason he will have many colleagues with whom he will sympathize. But it would be a mistake to employ such a man, as this will adversely affect the government of the domain. For if something occurs, the good and gentle man will be unable to either resist others' mistakes or encourage what is right. In this way a retainer may claim that affairs proceed without event, but this is the beginning of chaos. A military commander must keep his own eyes open.

This may seem to run counter to common sense, but it is typical of Warring States period–thinking, when it was believed that, contrary to times when all was in order, aggressive types should be employed during periods of conflict. Indeed, some discord was considered essential.

✦   ✦   ✦

Since time past, clans are usually overthrown by their chief retainers. A bright and thoughtful lord will direct his retainers himself, and will not simply entrust authority to others. If the lord entrusts his chief retainers to inform men of lower rank of commissions and stipends that he himself has granted, those who receive them will think that such favors have nothing to do with their lord, but rather come from the chief retainers. Thus it will be as though the lord were not there, and the authority of the chief retainers will increase day by day.

This was the admonishment Motonari gave to daimyo Ouchi Yoshitaka at the time he was under the latter's command. Yoshitaka controlled Hiroshima, Yamaguchi and Fukuoka, but his chief retainer, Sue Harukata, gradually strengthened his own influence. Despite Motonari's loyal words, Yoshitaka's power was wrested from him by his chief retainer, and a number of years later he was killed by Harukata. Harukata was attacked and defeated by the Mori clan forces, and chose suicide rather than capture.

The educated warlord would have read this advice in the works of the Chinese philosopher Han Fei-tzu: "When the chief retainers in authority exercise power as they please, those both inside and outside of the domain will follow suit."

⚜ ⚜ ⚜

The plans for the year are determined in the spring. The plans for the month are determined on the first day of that month. The plans for the day are determined when the cock crows.

Every year on New Year's Day, Motonari would wash his hands, rinse his mouth, and sit silently facing the east. One year, a close retainer, Kuriya Yajiro, called out, "It's time to go celebrate New Year's Day" Motonari, however, made no reply. Once again Yajiro called out, and this time Motonari silently stood up from his seat. After a short while, he called Yajiro over to him.

"Do you know why we celebrate New Year's Day?" he asked.

Yajiro was at a quandary as to how to respond, and simply bowed with his head and hands to the floor.

"The fools of this world," Motonari began, "feel that it's quite fine to bow in veneration to receive blessings, to ladle up spiced sake, and to pray for a long life and many descendants. But New Year's Day is not something for such happy-go-lucky people. At the very beginning of the year, you think thoroughly over your plans for the entire coming year. This is truly celebrating the New Year."

🔺　　🔺　　🔺

Do not be impressed with minor skills.

Motonari held that a person with great intentions should not be bothered with trifling skills. He should look steadily at what is in front of him, and not forget the issue at hand.

🔺　　🔺　　🔺

It is not enough to rely upon scholars. If they are given a stipend, there are many who will opine that their lord is clever and wise, will sputter out nothing but flattery, make literary works of the foolish and unintelligent words and deeds of their benefactor, and make him a laughing stock to later generations. No matter how many books of the sages they have read, they are generally not to be trusted.

27

One of Motonari's Confucian scholar retainers, Hokyo Esai, praised his master, remarking that his prestige and virtue shone throughout the Chugoku region, and that the people thought of him as equal to the ancient sage-kings of China. Motonari was not impressed, and quickly reprimanded Esai with the above words.

⁂

Since our domain has grown so large, our retainers have each become greatly prosperous, and obtained money and rice beyond what is ordinary in this world. Because of this, even the lower classes have become a bit too easy-going.

Motonari had enlarged his original fief from a small basin-like area north of Hiroshima to a huge domain consisting of ten provinces. Yet, he was not unconcerned about what the negative influences of all this wealth might be.

⁂

The person who makes light of the people will not become their lord. Take up the correct attitude so that you will not forget these words.

After subjugating the Chugoku region, Motonari gathered his generals and addressed them in this way. When he dispatched his generals to govern the provinces that had become his territory, he warned them not to exhibit the "extravagance of the victor."

Kikkawa Motoharu
(1530–1586)

MOTOHARU WAS THE SECOND SON of daimyo Mori Motonari, and was adopted into his mother's original clan, the Kikkawa. His younger brother Takakage was adopted by the Kobayakawa clan, and it was due to these two adoptions that the Mori dominion over the Chugoku region was all the more strengthened. When Toyotomi Hideyoshi attacked the Mori, Motoharu and Takakage put up an unbending resistance. When Hideyoshi's forces withdrew due to Nobunaga's assassination, however, Motoharu pursued them, while Takakage opposed this action. Thus, when Hideyoshi finally became the most powerful man in Japan, Motoharu unwillingly went into temporary retirement. He later died in action in Kyushu.

🌲　　🌲　　🌲

My desire to marry Nobutada's daughter is not because I have heard that his daughter is beautiful. It is because I have heard she is ugly.

As Motoharu became of age, his father Motonari began to think about having him get married, and dispatched retainer Kodama Naritada to his son to ask if he had a woman in mind. To this, Motoharu responded that the daughter of the retainer Kumadani Nobutada would be just fine. Naritada was taken aback, as this woman had a reputation of being quite ugly, but then thought that Motoharu must have gotten a false report and was thinking that the woman was actually somewhat of a beauty.

"If this is your wish," Naritada replied, "I will report it to your father right away. But are you sure that you'll have nothing to regret in this matter?"

"The reason I would like to marry Nobutada's daughter," Motoharu said with a laugh, "is not because I heard that she was beautiful. On the contrary, it's because I've heard that she's quite ugly. Being as ugly as she is, there will be no way that she can find a husband, and you can be sure that this will be a sad situation for her father Nobutada. Now if I take this woman as my wife, Nobutada—who is the finest general in all of the Chugoku region—will be grateful beyond measure, and would lay down his own life for me, to be sure. Even the strongest of our enemies would present no problem if he joined me at the vanguard of my father's troops."

Receiving this report, Motonari was overjoyed and encouraged the idea. And in the end, Kumadani Nobutada indeed performed great acts for the Mori clan.

The above relates an example of the "strategic marriage," but this concept was not restricted to either the Warring States period or the warrior class. The Ito clan, for example, was a wealthy family that flourished during the latter part of the Edo period (1615–1868), and among the articles in the "family constitution" was, "It is bad to have a beautiful woman as a wife. Consider it good if the woman simply has a good disposition."

The Ito felt that a beautiful woman would only eat up the clan's money, and that she would have no utilitarian value. Regardless of how this opinion might be judged today, it was, perhaps, a guide to survival toward the end of the shogunate government.

Another example related to this concept can be taken from the *Chuang Tzu*, a Chinese Taoist book written perhaps in the third or fourth century BC: "Long ago in China, the master of an inn had two concubines. One of them was extraordinarily beautiful, the other was horribly ugly, but it was the latter that the master treated with love and affection. A guest who happened to be staying at the inn thought this to be rather strange, and asked the master why he acted in this way. The master responded, "The beautiful woman has her nose in the air about her own beauty, and I have come to think that this is not very attractive. The ugly woman, on the other hand, thinks that she herself is not the least bit attractive, and this, I think, is not ugly at all."

In addition to his thoughts on marriage, Motoharu had this to say about bravery and wisdom.

> **The man who is brave, but who is lacking in wisdom may be effective as a soldier, but will lack the capacity to be a general. The man who would lead thousands of soldiers cannot be employed unless he exhibits wise strategies rather than some small degree of courage.**

Kobayakawa Takakage
(1533–1597)

KOBAYAKAWA TAKAKAGE was the third son of daimyo Mori Motonari, and younger brother of Kikkawa Motoharu. Adopted by the powerful Kobayakawa clan of the Hiroshima area, he furthered the influence of his father's clan in the Chugoku region. He at first fought against Oda Nobunaga and Toyotomi Hideyoshi, but later came to an agreement with the latter, and fought on his side. He eventually became one of the five members of Hideyoshi's Council of Elders, charged with being regents to Hideyoshi's heir.

🔱   🔱   🔱

If you have some pressing or urgent affair, write it down with a calm state of mind.

Once, Takakage ordered a scribe to take down an urgent letter. When the man picked up his brush in a rattled manner, Takakage reprimanded him with the above words.

🔱   🔱   🔱

Even if a samurai has wisdom and talent, if he is not liked by others, he will be clumsy in his affairs and will be estranged from the world at large.

From time to time, Takakage would leave the castle at night, and walk around the mansions of his retainers. When he passed by a house where people had gathered and were having a lively time, he would praise them good-humoredly. When he walked in front of a house that was deathly quiet, however, his eyebrows would narrow.

After you have made some important decision, you may have some regrets. This is because your intelligence is quick and nimble, and because you are wise enough so that when you hear one thing you understand two. So when you hear a man speak, you immediately make a decision on what is good and what is bad, and this is like water trying to find its own level. In this way, if you haven't fully considered a matter, there will be times when your decision may not be in accord with your true sentiments, and you may be caused to have some regrets.

Because my own particular genius is rather dull, when a man speaks, it is difficult for me to quickly determine the good from the bad. Thus, I have to exhaust what intelligence I have, think things through for a long time, and gradually discriminate what is right or wrong. Accordingly, I fully consider everything in my mind, eventually make a decision, and use every mental power I have on the matter. In this way I have had few regrets.

Takakage once said this to the resourceful military commander Kuroda Josui. Josui—who would later become the first daimyo of the Fukuoka Kuroda clan—and Takakage were on opposing sides during Hideyoshi's Chugoku campaign, but later both took part in the organization of the latter's general staff. Takakage was thirteen years older than Josui, and spoke these words out of a sense of loyalty. To Josui's questions, he added the following:

It's better to think for a long time, and to come to your decisions slowly. The essentials of discrimination are human-heartedness and love. Whenever you make decisions, if you discriminate using these two as your foundation, you will not be far from hitting what is right every time. Discrimination without human-heartedness and love will always be prejudiced, regardless of whatever genius, wisdom and skill may be in the mix.

When you state an opinion, the person who immediately agrees with you will likely be the person who ignores your opinion altogether. The man who listens carefully to another's words, thinks them over carefully, discusses the one or two points with which he cannot agree, and, after failing to understand the principles of the argument at first, finally finds them to be reasonable, will be the one who follows through with them afterward.

You should consider all the things that you find to be pleasant, as being nothing but poisons. And, you should consider those things that you think to be difficult, as being good medicine. Young people should take an interest in all things. In youth, there is still much time for such things, so there will always be moments for study. But when one grows old, he should spend more time in study. Because time is now short, and as there are few moments left, he should study all the more.

Life passes like a dream, and if one is not spoken of well by others, he should at least not be spoken of poorly.

Whenever you leave your gate, you should keep in mind the cross of crucifixion. Be of the mind that you will be hung on a cross if you are careless in your actions or speech, and do not be neglectful.

🔺   🔺   🔺

Practicing the Way of Tea is for the purpose of escaping the complications of society's dust, and approaching our abodes in the crags and fields; it is for the purpose of following after the leisure of the streams, clouds, birds and fish, and for putting our minds at ease. This is what I thought, and so practiced it with great relish. However, when I looked carefully at the people in this world who love it the most, I found that they often discussed the high or low value of tea utensils, or that they either praised or were envious of those who are virtuosos at buying utensils worth a thousand strings of cash for only a hundred, or that they wished that they might buy something at a cheap price and sell it for a dear one. Such people have lost the truest significance of Tea. Even if this were not so, men's minds are easily moved by material things.

🔺   🔺   🔺

Once, when Takakage was staying in Kyoto, he had need of an accountant and so employed a certain townsman, and attached him as a subordinate official to his retainer Ukai Shin'emon. His stay in Kyoto passed without event, and, as the closing account of his expenses showed a remainder of eight *kan*,[2] the townsman entered that amount into the books. Ukai Shin'emon was impressed with the townsman's ability, and considered praising

---

2. *Kan*: a unit of money.

him highly. This he then reported to Takakage. Contrary to his expectations, Takakage was enraged.

"If there had not been enough funds, I could understand," he stormed. "But what is this business of a remainder? Do you think this money fell from heaven or bubbled up from the earth? There's no doubt that either he haggled and got the price lowered when payments were made, or that he didn't pay the full price. Doing so, he has covered me with shame. He should have paid out fully and come up with insufficient funds, but instead has accounted us with a remainder. What a detestable fellow! Behead the man!"

Everyone was shocked, and got through the difficulty by revising the accounts to show an insufficiency of funds.

Takeda Shingen
(1521–1573)

IN AN AGE OF REMARKABLE MEN, Takeda Shingen was one of the most remarkable. The second son of the ruler of the province of Kai, he usurped his father's position at the age of twenty-one, and by the age of thirty-five controlled the neighboring province of Shinano. From that time on, he fought with the Hojo, Imagawa and Tokugawa clans, and then made alliances with them. His most famous battles—which continued for over twenty years— were in Kawanakajima[1] with Uesugi Kenshin, lord of Echigo Province and Shingen's main rival. Shingen was considered by many to be the man who would eventually conquer and unite the country, but he was struck by a rifle ball during the siege of Noda Castle,[2] and died three days later. Romantic tradition has it that he was resting on a camp seat, listening to the sound of a flute being played inside the castle, when a sniper was able to hit his mark. His death was kept a secret for some time, and he was buried three years later.

🔺　　　🔺　　　🔺

Men are your castles; men are your stone walls; men are your moats. Fellow feeling is your ally; enmity is your enemy.

---

1. Kawanakajima in Shinano Province was the site of a series of battles (1553–1564) between Takeda Shingen and Uesugi Kenshin. The end results were not conclusive, but the battles became a popular subject for epic poetry and prints.
2. An alternative theory is that his demise was due to a sudden illness.

The above statement is famous for having been Shingen's motto. He firmly believed that people would be his greatest strength, and throughout his life never built a castle in his domain of Kai Province. He placed great importance on the governance within the domain, and as the people of his fief progressed, they became his intangible stronghold. When one of his elder retainers proposed that a castle should be built, he responded,

A lieutenant-general will build a castle and must hold out there until the main forces arrive, but what will a commander-in-chief do if he relies on a castle? A man who intends to control the entire country must take great care of his human resources, and must place more importance in the construction of his mind than in the construction of castles.

Wu Tzu (440–381 BC), the famous Chinese strategist, put it this way: "If the people of one domain consider their lord to be a good one, and the people of another domain do not, and the two countries enter hostilities, the former will have already won."

⚜   ⚜   ⚜

To perform actions on your own is of no use. And to perform some action on your own while in the command of foot soldiers will be the same as the foot soldiers having no commander at all. In this way, you will not be able to determine the winning course of a battle, and your forces will be defeated.

Shingen spoke these words to his retainer Tada Kuzo when he made him a general of infantrymen.

⚜   ⚜   ⚜

A warrior should know that the man who can ride the most unruly of horses is the man fit to be a general.

Shingen wrote this in the form of a poem when he had dispatched a man to the northern part of Japan to purchase horses. That a general should be able to mount the most unruly of unruly horses refers, of course, to the fact that a true leader must be able to deal with and use well the most unruly of his fellow men.

To cut down a sour persimmon and graft a sweet persimmon on to its trunk is the deed of a neophyte. A man above the middling, and especially a man who would rule the nation will find the best use of a sour persimmon just as it is.

Again, this is a metaphor for best using every man in terms of his own character, be it rough or easy-going, sweet or sour. In the *Analects of Confucius* we read: "The Gentleman[3] is not a utensil." This means that the Gentleman is not a machine to be useful for only one purpose. He is something larger than that.

You can know what a man's qualities will be from an early age. If you are telling stories to children about warriors' deeds, you will be able to determine four types of child. The first will simply look and listen with open mouth to the man who is talking; the second will strain his ears, and listen with downcast eyes; the third will look at the speaker's face, will smile a little, and look as though he understands; the fourth will listen and get up and leave his seat.

Now the first child, who listened in an absentminded way, will, just as his mind seems, be unable to discern the details of a situation, no matter how many times he participates on

---

3. The Gentleman (君子): the Confucian ideal.

the battlefield. He will not have fitting retainers, and will not have friends who will give him differing opinions.

Now the second child, the one who strains his ears to listen, will become a man who understands what it is to be a warrior. He will be like Yokota of Bitchu; Hara of Mino, Obata of Yamashio, Tada of Awaji, and Yamamoto Kansuke.

The third, the child who listened to the stories while laughing with an amused expression, will surely be praised for his martial deeds at a later date, but will go too far, will become proud and haughty, and detested by others.

The fourth child, who got up and left his seat, will—eight or nine times out of ten—become a coward.

When you think about employing samurai, it is essential that you act just as you would when you seek something to drink if your throat is dry.

It is good to hire and train even a man who is a bit slow.

Generally speaking, people become either good or bad according to their upbringing. For the children of daimyo, it is good to have them listen to talks about a general's deportment and actions from the time they are seven or eight years old until they are twelve or thirteen. For children of lower ranks, it is best to speak to them about the courageous martial acts of strong men, and of prudence in their own behavior. By and large, what a person has heard and been trained in up to the time he is twelve or thirteen will not be lost on him for the rest of his life.

The time when a youth's voice changes is an extremely important one. A boy who mixes with good companions will

turn out well, while one who associates with bad fellows will turn out poorly.

Shingen was interested in and careful to nurture and cultivate all of his retainers, not just the strong and wise ones. He was also very careful to educate the young members of his fief, and this is reflected in the following statement.

🔺   🔺   🔺

Ninety-nine out of a hundred warriors who praise others will turn out to be bad men. They will likely be one out of four types: insincere, those who rely on their wits, thieves or flatterers.

Shingen is said to have admired men who were not afraid to make enemies when they spoke their convictions.

🔺   🔺   🔺

Wind. Forest. Fire. Mountain.

This was the foundation of Shingen's military strategy, and he had the four characters (風, 林, 火, 山) affixed to his banners. They are said to express the deepest principles of the martial arts: activity and inactivity, straightforwardness and the unexpected, and freedom of transformation. The reference is to the words of fifth century BC Chinese strategist, Sun Tzu, author of *The Art of War*: "His speed must be like the wind; his calm like a forest; his aggression like fire, and his stability like a mountain."

🔺   🔺   🔺

Generally speaking, it is best to win fifty percent of your battles; seventy percent is all right; and one hundred percent is the worst. With only fifty percent, you will have more incentive; with seventy percent, you will become lazy; with one hundred percent, you will become prideful.

When it comes to battle, until one turns forty, a man should think only of winning. After forty, he should think only of not losing. A man around the age of twenty, however, should not lose to an opponent of lower rank, but should not overwhelm him.

Shingen would have been familiar with these quotes from Lao Tzu, the fifth century BC Chinese philosopher:

"The hard and rigid are the followers of death;
The pliant and flexible are the followers of life.
For this reason, if weapons are too rigid, they will not last.
If trees are too rigid,
    they will be cut down and used as furnishings."

"The man who makes himself a good warrior
    does not stride fiercely forward with a spear."

Everyone says that when you lose to an army you should not have lost to, or when your clan is destroyed by a clan that it

should not have been destroyed by, it is the Will of Heaven.[4]
I myself do not consider such things to be the Will of Heaven,
but rather the result of doing things badly. If you do things
well, you are unlikely to be defeated.

☖   ☖   ☖

A man wants fame to the extent that he does not get results.

☖   ☖   ☖

If a man does the things he finds unpleasant, rather than the
things he wants to do, he should do well in life.

Shingen made this remark one night when he had sat together with a number of his retainers. When he asked, "Do you know
the method whereby a man will make no mistakes throughout his
entire life, regardless of rank?" no one had an answer. The above
statement was his response to their silence.

☖   ☖   ☖

A man having Learning[5] is like a tree having branches and
leaves. He should not be without it. Still, this is not a matter
of just reading books. Learning is something we study to in-
tegrate with our own particular path. First, if a man is born to
a warrior's clan, regardless of rank, he should approach those
men renowned for their military accomplishments. If he listens to but one item a day, thirty items a month, and so learns

---

4. Lit., Heaven's command (天命).
5. Learning (学 or 学問): less in a scholastic sense than in a good foundation of Confucianism.

43

three hundred and sixty things in a year, he will be far and away superior to the man he was the year before. In this way, if you abandon your old self, and add on the good of others, you should suffer few indignities. If a man were to penetrate this principle completely, I would praise him and call him wise, even if he could not read a single Chinese character.

To take a number of provinces is a matter of good fortune. Men who united the entire nation were Minamoto no Yorito-mo [1147–1199], Hojo Yasutoki [1183–1242], and Ashikaga Takauji [1305–1358]. Each of these men had the good fortune to realize the great desire of warrior clans. But before their good fortune, each of these also passed through extraordinari-ly difficult times. There is also the example of the great lord Minamoto no Yoshitsune, who went through great hardships and was famous in battle, but wound up with only the prov-ince of Iyo. In this way you can see that good fortune is some-thing not easily understood, and that one should be prudent and not stain oneself in battle to the very end. If you maintain the Way, take up your weapons, gain a long life and entrust things to destiny, in the end, you may naturally see the em-pire appear right before your eyes. For example, even though you may be in a hurry, it will be difficult to make spring leap into fall. Because this principle and the matter of luck are not easily understood, men desire large fiefs and great provinces, turn their backs on the lord to whom they owe so much, and act without righteousness. And even if they do accomplish something, if the time is not right, they meet with untoward deaths. There are many, many examples of this in both the past and the present, and it is something truly to be feared.

As might be expected of the man who stated that "men are your castle," there are many anecdotes about how Shingen put people to use. He gave serious consideration to matching his subordinates. Baba Nobufusa, for example, was a man of few words, and Shingen paired him with the eloquent speaker, Naito Masamori; with the hot-tempered and ferociously brave Yamagata Masakage, he assigned the cautious Kosaka Masanobu. Once, he ordered a bold fellow and a very mild man to take a post together, saying, "Neither of those fellows will think that taking second place to the other is somehow an embarrassment, so I think that they will work together as harmoniously as fire and water."

A certain Iwama Okurazaemon had the reputation of being a coward. On the battlefield, he was of no use, but Shingen assigned him to the position of "hidden overseer," a sort of watchdog who spied on the evil deeds of the clan's retainers. When Shingen assigned the man to this role, he threatened him with death if he was informed about such deeds only after they had happened. Shaken by these words, Iwama reported everything to Shingen in detailed accounts, and thus was a very useful man.

A ronin by the name of Hida Take'emon was hoping to be taken into Shingen's service. When the clan administrator asked him what kind of meritorious deeds he had achieved, however, Take'emon only spoke about his weak points. The person who had introduced him got angry, and lamented that he had sponsored the man, but Take'emon only waited imperturbed for the outcome.

When Shingen received the administrator's report, he said, "There's no doubt that this man is quite suitable," and employed him right away. Later, the man's deeds earned him the nickname Shingen's Demon Take'emon.

🔱　　　🔱　　　🔱

Whenever Shingen employed someone, he would give him plenty of money and clothing, but would not present him with a fief until he had taken full measure of the man. Had Shingen immediately made the presentation of a fief and later understood that the man was unfit, he would have had to take back the land. This would have caused harm to the man in question, and Shingen himself would be seen to lack judgment. Being prudent in this matter, he at first proffered material goods, but not land itself.

🔱　　　🔱　　　🔱

Both before and after Shingen took to the field, he would gather his generals together, and hold a council where it was his custom to have each man discuss the day's battle, particularly its aftermath. Listening silently, he would make his own critique.

🔱　　　🔱　　　🔱

The times for arriving and leaving one's work in the Takeda clan were unconventional. In other clans, a warrior would arrive at his post every morning, but in the Takeda clan, each person would arrive at the time of his own discretion, having notified his colleagues in advance. Of course, some coordination and control was imposed, but it was not bound by form, and the aim was to have each person work positively according to his own spontaneity. It is interesting that what we now call "flex time" was put into practice over four hundred years ago.

Takeda Nobushige
(1525–1561)

NOBUSHIGE WAS THE younger brother of Takeda Shingen. When their father seemed ready to transfer the headship of the clan to Nobushige, the latter did not take it. Though he led a life that was naturally hidden by Shingen's shadow, he was, in fact, a loyal man who served his older brother, and died in battle at Kawanakajima.

🔺　　🔺　　🔺

Though a man be a good friend, do not converse with him about topics such as debauchery or lewdness. Should he begin to speak about such things, get up and leave in an unobtrusive way.

The phrase *mara kyodai* (魔羅兄弟) means the relationship between two men who understand each other's weak points is a strong one. But can a relationship in which one man is in an inferior position truly be strong in the end? Nobushige, one of the most earnest men of the Warring States period, exquisitely demonstrated that it can.

Nobushige was perhaps overly careful, and he was constantly concerned that some incident might come between him and his older brother. In this regard, a sentence that appears in *The Ninety-nine Articles*, a set of guiding precepts to live by that he left to his son, goes as follows. "No matter how much Lord Shingen looks upon you with approval, you must not become accustomed to such treatment, and try to become informal with him."

Baba Nobufusa
(1515–1575)

ACCOUNTED AS ONE OF THE "four great retainers" of the Takeda, Nobufusa served three generations of that clan's lords. During his life he fought over thirty battles, in which he was renowned for both his boldness and skill. He died at the battle of Nagashino after having his lord, Takeda Katsuyori, escape.

🔺　　🔺　　🔺

A battle is something that involves innumerable changes and infinite varieties, and often goes contrary to whatever you may have planned beforehand. Thus it is essential to exert yourself, entrusting those places that go contrary to your plans to themselves. If you are perplexed and confused when things don't proceed as you have thought they might, you will suffer a great defeat with humiliating results.

Nobufusa spent nearly his entire life on the battlefield, so these words are not simply theoretical; they derive from long practical observation. In *The Art of War* by Chinese strategist Sun Tzu, we read: "Listen, the shape of battle imitates water. Water avoids the high, and proceeds toward the low; battle avoids the true, and attacks the false. Water establishes its flow according to the land; battle establishes its victory according to its opponent. Thus, as water has no set form, battle has no set method. The man who can transform his strategies according to the moves of his opponent has godlike abilities."

You may do great deeds or become imprudent according to your courage or cowardice, but there is one thing you should keep in mind. Since I was young, there have been five criterions I have tried to meet, and because of them I have not been negligent.

The first is that on days when your own troops would appear more courageous than the enemy, you should commit yourself to take the initiative in battle. But on days when your troops appear to waver and fall back, when one or two men advance and die meaninglessly, it either gives the enemy more opportunities, or at least is a mistake which allows them to steal the march on you.

The second is to become on good terms with a warrior who has participated in a number of battles, to use him as a model, and to make an effort not to come short of that model.

The third is that if the ornaments on the enemy's helmets are facing downward, and their banners unmoving, then you should understand that this is a strong enemy. If helmet ornaments are facing upward and banners are moving, then this is a weak enemy and it is best to ready your spears.

The fourth is to observe the enemy's spears. If they are pointed upward, they are a weak enemy; if they are lowered, they are a strong one. If the points of the spears are lined up, they will be long-handled spears and thus indicative of a troop of foot-soldiers. If some are long and some short, they will be held by men of the samurai class. Your own samurai should then be armed with spears.

The fifth is that if an opponent is highly spirited, you should receive him with restraint, and, when you see that he is weakening, strike at him all at once.

✲   ✲   ✲

If someone promotes only those things the lord finds acceptable, and never remonstrates with him at all, you should watch that man carefully.

✲   ✲   ✲

Among Shingen's generals, Nobufusa was said to be the most taciturn. But because of this, he was all the more a radical man of action. During the campaign in Suruga, the Takeda forces attacked Imagawa Ujizane, head of the Imagawa clan, and their victory was assured. At this point, Shingen ordered his soldiers to enter the Imagawa mansion immediately and loot it of its treasures. As soon as Nobufusa heard this, however, he galloped to the mansion, set it on fire, and burned it to the ground. He was concerned, he said later, that looting the mansion would earn his master the dishonor of being known as a "Master of Greed."

Nobufusa often pointed out that, according to the situation, there is always the danger of falling into a subjective judgment. The following anecdote gives an example of this.

A certain man was once talking along in a gossipy way. "It seems as though townsfolk are convinced that warriors who perform great exploits are quite strong. I read something written by a townsman concerning Akamatsu Mitsusuke's murdering the shogun Yoshinori," he laughed. "It said he must have had the strength of three hundred men."

Nobufusa did not smile at all, but said, "If a warrior said something about a merchant, it would be a wrong assumption as well. You probably think that this townsman was amusing, but you should never speak thoughtlessly about things beyond your ken."

Kosaka Masanobu
(1527–1578)

ONE OF TAKEDA SHINGEN'S "four great retainers," Masanobu was deputy governor of Omoro Castle, and governor of Kaizu Castle. A prudent advocate for the Takeda clan, he looked scrupulously at each state of affairs, and remonstrated against dangerous adventurism. He is possibly the author of the original manuscript of the *Koyogunkan*, a chronicle of Takeda Shingen and his times.

🔥　　🔥　　🔥

Three things you should not push on others are medicine, horses, and *fugu*.[1] If any of these were to cause damage, it would be unseemly if you did not commit ritual suicide. But whether they cause a death or not, there is nothing, after all, that you should keep your distance from more than these.

Masanobu admonished thus Shingen's son, Takeda Katsuyori.

🔥　　🔥　　🔥

When you employ a man, use him for his employable traits; do not criticize him for his petty flaws.

No matter how strong your intention, if you do not have resources or a design that you can make concrete, all your

---

1. *Fugu*: a kind of blowfish. The meat is very white, delicate and delicious, but if not prepared expertly, can cause paralysis and death.

intention will come to nothing. Yet if you do something concretely but without resources, you will have no result. You are walking along a road, for example, and come to the bank of a large river. The water has risen, you are not familiar with the shallows, and thus you are hesitant to cross as you might be swept away in the current. Here, your intention is to cross over, but no matter how strong your intention, if you have no means to cross, it comes to nothing. Accordingly, you use some discretion: as you are not familiar with the river yourself, you make the rounds looking for someone who is, and a guide will eventually appear voluntarily. This is resources.

In his youth, Masanobu was so careful to avoid dangerous situations, his nickname was "Fleeing Danjo."[2] His character is clearly expressed in the above words.

🏵   🏵   🏵

The decorum of every samurai should be like the way you wear both long and short swords in your sash. If you are too ostentatious, and always ready for a fight, it will be like wearing naked blades at your side; if you are too "good," and do not have the right mental attitude, it will be like wearing a sword without an edge, which you might as well throw away.

Tsuchiya Masatsugu, one of Shingen's commanders, once asked Masanobu, "When a samurai is too fond of the Way of the Warrior, he'll get into fights too often; but if he's too affable and friendly, he neglects our Way. What about this?" The above was Masanobu's response.

---

2. Danjo: another of Masanobu's names.

Uesugi Kenshin
(1530–1578)

"YOUR DESTINY IS IN HEAVEN; your armor is in your mind." Due to the death of his father, Nagao Tamekage, and the incompetence of his elder brother, Masakage, Kenshin left home to become a monk at the age of eleven. After traveling over a number of provinces, he was advised to return home by Usami Sadayuki, one of his father's retainers. He did so, and at the age of thirteen, deposed his elder brother and took the reins of the Uesugi clan. The rest of his life was consumed by constant warfare and campaigns, his most notable opponent having been Takeda Shingen, with whom he fought every year for a decade at Kawanakajima. He became a Buddhist monk in 1552, but did not abandon his role as commander-in-chief of his clan's forces.

✦　　　✦　　　✦

I'm tired beyond measure. Let me rest a little, then I'll get going.

After his father's death, the Nagao clan had split into quarreling factions in the competition for the control of the province of Echigo. During the latter half of the Muromachi period (1333–1573), upon the death of a local daimyo, others in the area would either compete or cooperate in the struggle to fill the void. The Nagao clan, which had already wrested power from the Uesugi, was no exception.

Pursued by other factions of his clan, Kenshin sought refuge at Tochio Castle, but his brother Masakage received intelligence of this and laid siege to the castle with seven thousand men.

Kenshin's close retainers advised him to go out immediately and attack, but he responded, "The enemy will withdraw soon. It would be better to pursue and attack them then." He had correctly perceived that the opposing forces had brought few provisions, and did not intend a prolonged engagement; and indeed, the enemy began to withdraw that very night. Seeing their enemies' unguarded position, the troops in the castle hurried out in pursuit, and crushed their foe. As the routed enemy made for the pass on Mount Yone, Kenshin's troops gathered at the foot of the mountain and were ready to make chase. At this point, however, Kenshin uttered the above quote, went into a small hut at the side of the road, and went to sleep. No matter how his generals tried to arouse him, he would not get up. To the astonishment of his troops, he simply lay there asleep.

Once he thought the enemy had crossed over the pass, however, Kenshin jumped up, ordered his men to start out, and ascended the pass with a single advance. The enemy troops were attacked as they descended the mountain, and were killed in great numbers. Thus was Kenshin, who had waited for just the right juncture, handed a momentous victory.

This story was likely embellished in the years after the event, but it illustrates Kenshin's insightful strategies. In fact, he was only nineteen or twenty at the time. With this victory, he pacified the opposing forces, became the governor of the castles at Mount Kasuga, and was later to make peace with Masakage.

It is not my intention to attack those I perceive to be in adversity.

The rivalry between Kenshin and Takeda Shingen was the subject of *Kawanakajima kassen* (The battle of Kawanakajima), one of the great epic poems about the Warring States period, written by the scholar Rai San'yo (1780–1832). The famous single combat between the two at Kawanakajima took place in 1561, when Kenshin was thirty-two, and Shingen forty-one. This was one year after the twenty-year-old Oda Nobunaga defeated daimyo Imagawa Yoshimoto at Okehazama.

One day in 1573, Kenshin was just eating a meal when he was informed that Shingen had become sick and died on the road. Without thinking, he dropped his chopsticks and spit out the boiled rice he had been eating. "Well, this is a terrible shame," he lamented. "What a pity to have such a great general die on me." Moreover, he mourned for his rival for three days, forbidding any music or merriment.

One of his chief retainers suggested that they take advantage of this opportunity, and invade Shingen's domains. Kenshin rejected this, and made no move to advance. He fully understood that after Shingen's death, the Takeda clan would begin to waver, and there would be a number of opportunities for him later. But at his great rival's demise, he simply spoke out with the above quote, and dispatched no troops.

Making something up and receiving empty fame amounts to nothing. Your mind is your own witness, is it not? On the contrary, though in fact you achieve great works, yet your name remains unknown, if your own mind bears witness, you should hold no grudges.

A strange rumor had made its way from the Takeda domains in Kai Province to Uesugi Kenshin. In a battle that had just occurred at Kawanakajima, a certain Abe Kaga, a page to Shingen's son Katsuyori, had killed a courageous warrior of the Uesugi by the name of Ochiai Hikosuke, and Shingen had rewarded the page for this feat.

But far from having been killed, this Ochiai was quite alive and well. Very clearly, Abe Kaga had fabricated this great deed, and Shingen, unaware of the facts, had rewarded him.

Kenshin then met with Ochiai Hikosuke, and stated the above bluntly.

🌲　　　🌲　　　🌲

Functioning on the battlefield is the ordinary course for the warrior. It is the same as tilling the field for the farmer. The warrior considers it best when his everyday manners are good and his sense of decency is correct. He does not consider it best to receive many fiefs and a high position by martial feats alone.

Kenshin felt strongly that a man was to be employed or promoted because of his character rather than just for his capacity in his everyday work.

🌲　　　🌲　　　🌲

Your destiny is in Heaven; your armor is in your mind; your achievements are in your feet. You should always fight with this in mind, hold the enemy in the palm of your hand, and thus suffer no loss. If you fight without a thought for your life, you will live; if you fight thinking only to say alive, you will surely die. If you give up hope of ever returning home once you leave the gate, you will come home once more; if you only think of returning, you'll not see your home again. You may think only that your life is insecure, and no doubt about it, that goes without saying, but the Way of the Warrior

is not in thinking about insecurity; it is only in thinking that you are secure in the Way yourself.

These were among the precepts posted on the wall in the castle at Mount Kasuga.

Frost fills the camp in the pure autumn air;
Files of geese pass the moon at midnight.
The mountains of Echigo merge with the scenery of Noto.
Still, still, on this campaign I think of home.

This poem was written while Kenshin was attacking the strategic Nanao Castle in the Noto Peninsula in 1576. Kenshin's range of influence stretched from Ugo and Uzen in the north, Kozuke in the south, and Noto in the west,[1] but his enemies in Noto had the backing of Oda Nobunaga. The siege of the castle lasted over a month, but it finally fell to the Uesugi forces. On the night of September 13, Kenshin held a moon-viewing party inside the castle, and recited the above poem to his guests.

The following are among Kenshin's clan precepts.

- When your mind is not occupied by things, it will be expansive and your body will be serene.
- When your mind is without conceit, love and respect will not be lacking.

---

1. The current prefectures of Akita and Yamagata, Gunma, and Ishikawa respectively.

- When your mind is without desire, you will behave righteously.
- When your mind is without self-centeredness, you will have no doubts.
- When your mind is without pride, you will respect others.
- When your mind is without twisted views, you will educate others.
- When your mind is without covetousness, you will not flatter others.
- If your mind is without anger, your words will be harmonious.
- When your mind is patient, you will put your affairs in order.
- When your mind is not clouded, it will be at peace.
- When your mind is courageous, you will have no regrets.
- If your mind is not base, you will not like making requests to others.
- When your mind possesses filial piety, you will be rich with loyalty.
- When your mind is without self-praise, you will know the good in others.
- When your mind is without confusion, you will not lay blame elsewhere.

⚜   ⚜   ⚜

If I am there, Bishamonten[2] will help out. If I am not there, Bishamonten will not be there either. If I pray to Bishamonten a hundred times, Bishamonten will likely bow in veneration to me fifty or maybe thirty times.

---

2. Bishamonten: Buddhist god of defensive warfare. He holds a lance (of wisdom) in one hand, and a stupa in the other, and his messenger animal is a centipede. He is often shown fully armored, and crushing a demon underfoot.

Kenshin believed in the Buddhist deity Bishamonten (毘沙門天), and affixed the Chinese character 毘 on his battle banners. At the time of some momentous event, he would gather his retainers together in the Bishamon temple inside the castle grounds, and make vows to this god.

Once Kenshin was in a hurry to dispatch a secret agent to a neighboring province. He was supposed to have the agent make vows at the Bishamon temple before leaving, but there was no time for this, so he had the man make his vows before him instead. When his elder retainers protested and said that this went against precedent, Kenshin laughed, and stated the above. He was, indeed, a deeply spiritual person, and not a run-of-the-mill believer.

⚜　　⚜　　⚜

Do not concern yourself with Heaven and Hell
　　Straight ahead is the pale morning moon.
Set your mind there
　　without a cloud in sight.

By 1577, Kenshin had nearly pacified the Noto area, and, determined to enter Kyoto, was making his preparations for his strategy to eliminate Nobunaga. He passed away, however, in March of the following year at the relatively young age of forty-nine. His respected rival Shingen had preceded him in death five years before. Above is Kenshin's death poem.

Ryuzoji Takanobu
(1529–1584)

TAKANOBU WAS THE grandson of Ryuzoji Iekane, who first established his clan as the rulers of a domain in Kyushu. Iekane had wrested the fief away from his former masters, the Shoni, in typical *gekokujo*—retainer overcoming lord—fashion. Takanobu had originally wanted to become a Buddhist monk, but left religious life at age eighteen. He was constantly at war with his neighbors, ever trying to increase his possessions, and in 1553 he captured the castle at Saga in Hizen Province. He was a courageous leader and won many battles, but was defeated and killed in action while fighting against the Shimazu clan. Takanobu's son, Masaie, was more famous for being overweight[1] and incompetent than clever or martial, and ceded his domain to the Nabeshima—descendants of the Shoni—only three years after receiving it as his own.

If you think something over for too long, your thoughts will grow stale.

Takanobu was in conflict with his neighbors all of his life, and did not have the leisure for long deliberative thought. This axiom may have been instilled in him during his early brief career study-

---

1. In the book *Hagakure*, there is a story about Masaie being so fat that after a game of *go* with Hideyoshi, he was unable to get to his feet, and had to crawl away on all fours. It was also said that he was unable to mount his own horse without the help of a number of his retainers. One imagines how his father, Takanobu, would have felt about this.

ing Buddhism, which places more emphasis on intuition than on long cogitation. Just as likely, however, the source of this concept will have been the political and military circumstances within which Takanobu lived. No sooner had he defeated the remnants of the Shoni in their attempt to regain their former possession, than he had to deal with the Arima, Omura and Otomo clans.

Thus, to be long in making a decision, to leisurely think over all of the pluses and minuses of an action, will only lead to no action at all, and so disaster. A Japanese saying has it that "to think over something unskillfully is the same as stopping work,"[2] and this is considered to be applicable whenever conflict is involved, be it on the *go* board or at a kendo match.

---

2. 下手の考え休むに似たり. *Heta no kangae yasumu ni nitari.*

Imagawa Yoshimoto
(1519–1560)

YOSHIMOTO WAS THE DESCENDANT of a line of illustrious warriors, who claimed to be in the family line of the Seiwa Genji, descendants of the emperor Seiwa. Yoshimoto became a monk in his youth, but had to take over his family's domains after the death of his elder brother. A talented general and politician, he fought against the Takeda and Hojo clans, and eventually brought the three strategically important provinces of Mikawa, Suruga and Totomi under his control. In 1559 he began a campaign to conquer Owari Province. The following year, however, in a moment of miscalculation and perhaps hubris, he was defeated and killed during a surprise attack by a small force under the command of Oda Nobunaga. Yoshimoto's son, Ujizane, to whom the quote below is addressed, possessed neither the talent nor ambition of his father. Effortlessly defeated twice by Takeda Shingen, Ujizane appealed to Tokugawa Ieyasu for refuge, and was awarded a small pension. He eventually made his way to Kyoto, became a monk, and died at the age of seventy-seven.

🔱　　🔱　　🔱

You've already become an adult, but have not yet lost your childish mind. You engage in cock fights or dog races, but have completely ignored what should be your primary studies: the cultural and the martial. If you do not mend your ways now, it is inevitable that our domains will be overthrown and that our clan will be ruined.

Oda Nobunaga
(1534–1582)

THE SON OF A MINOR warlord from Owari Province, Nobunaga became the most powerful and feared general of the era, ruthlessly eliminating one rival after another, starting with the assassination of his younger brother, whom he suspected of disloyalty. When his father died, he inherited the clan leadership at age sixteen. At twenty-seven, he killed the prominent warlord Imagawa Yoshimoto; and at thirty-one drove warlord Saito Tatsuoki out of the province of Mino. Throughout his career, he made alliances by marriage, but when the time was right, turned on his former allies and destroyed them. He installed and at first supported the shogun Ashikaga Yoshiaki, but later drove him from Kyoto when the latter started moving away from his influence. Nobunaga seemed well on his way to subjugating the entire country, and now turned his attention to the west of Japan. On June 21, 1582, however, he was betrayed and attacked while resting in the Honnoji temple in Kyoto, by one of his most noted generals, Akechi Mitsuhide. Retreating to the rear of the burning temple, he committed ritual suicide. His body was never found.

🔥　　🔥　　🔥

A true military commander shows only the exterior of his hand, and is not made light of by his subordinates.

Nobunaga was not hesitant to give out awards for meritorious work, but he constantly did things that others did not expect. For example, to the man who anticipated receiving the gift of a sword, Nobunaga would present a short-sleeved kimono; to the man who thought for sure that he would be given a horse, he would present money. Such actions were examples of the "improper awards" mentioned in *The Art of War* by Chinese strategist Sun Tzu.

But it was not just with his commanders and subordinates that he manifested this style of doing things. Concerning the art of war, he said,

> In attacking an enemy, you do not make your attack where and when he would expect one to be reasonable. You attack when he least expects it. How will you succeed if you go out to where he is waiting for you? A half-baked intelligence is the worst intelligence of all.

🌲   🌲   🌲

> The fifty years of a mans life,
>   Compare this with taking the nation:[1]
> A dream, an illusion.
>   One born to life
>   Will surely perish.

This quotation, from the Noh play *Atsumori*, was a favorite of Nobunaga's. He chanted it and performed the attending dance before defeating daimyo Imagawa Yoshimoto at the Battle of Okehazama. The story has it that in 1560, Yoshimoto set out from present-day Shizuoka with a huge army of forty thousand men, his plan being to pacify Owari Province and then to move on to the west. In historical fact, his army seems to have numbered

---

1. The nation, 天下. In some texts this is 化転, meaning to receive the Buddhist teaching, and to leave the bad for the good.

only twenty-five thousand but it was a large assembly of troops nonetheless. Nobunaga was to meet this powerful force with no more than four thousand warriors, and ordinarily, his prospects of victory would have been nonexistent.

Yoshimoto entered Okazaki on May 16. On May 18 he invaded Owari Province. He was twenty-seven years old. At Owari Castle in Kiyosu, he was now informed hourly of the local troops' defeats, yet did not call a war council. When his elder retainers offered to go out in advance of the inevitable siege of the castle, Nobunaga did not give them permission, or orders for any attack.

When night fell, Nobunaga ordered his chief retainers to evacuate the castle. The retainers, having up to this point put their fates in Nobunaga's hands, could do nothing more than obey. But the fact was that Nobunaga had already determined his own intention, and was just waiting for the right moment.

At two in the morning on May 19, Nobunaga got up and put on his armor. He saddled his horse, ate a bowl of rice gruel, and picked up a small Noh hand drum. He then chanted and danced to the aforementioned lines from *Atsumori* three times. Then, leaping onto his horse, he dashed out of the castle gate. The men who followed behind were only fifty in number, but more subordinates rushed to join the ranks. By the time they reached Atsuta Shrine in Nagoya, they were two hundred. Dawn began to break.

At last, about two thousand troops had gathered around him, and they began to advance toward the east. Yet, the stronghold of their allies seemed to have fallen, and black smoke rose far in the distance. They were informed that the commander Sakuma Morishige had fallen in battle, and soon learned that the main Imagawa force was resting at the ravine at Dengakuhazama.

Nobunaga detoured and traveled unseen over a mountain path, and came out over the ravine about noon. Just then, the sky suddenly grew dark, and a heavy rain began to fall. The Imagawa forces had been eating their midday meal, basking in the victories they had had since the beginning of the campaign, but were now running back and forth to get out of the sudden rainstorm. At this point, the Oda forces attacked, shouting their battle cries.

Imagawa Yoshimoto was struck down and killed in the melee that followed, and Nobunaga took one more step on the way to national supremacy.

🔥　　🔥　　🔥

When you employ a man, select him according to his abilities or the lack thereof. What difference does it make if he is a new or old retainer?

Oda Nobunaga promoted Kinoshita Tokichiro[2] to a responsible position, although a number of people were not pleased by this, and often slandered the newcomer. But Nobunaga paid no heed to them, and simply responded with the above words.

🔥　　🔥　　🔥

The common man cannot know what is in the mind of a commanding general.

In 1575, daimyo Uesugi Kenshin attacked the Noto area. Nobunaga went to aid his allies there, but his forces were inadequate and he returned without result. There were no doubt complaints about this failure, intimating cowardice or perhaps selfishness on his part. What Nobunaga had in mind, however, was an ancient Chinese saying and anecdote from the Chinese historical text, *Records of the Grand Historian*: "In the latter part

---

2. Kinoshita Tokichiro. Later named Toyotomi Hideyoshi. Born a peasant, he became the most powerful man in Japan after Nobunaga's death.

of the Ch'in dynasty, a farmer by the name of Ch'en Sheng paused with what he was doing for a moment and muttered, "Even if I become a great man, I will not forget my companions." Those of his companions who heard this laughed and chided him. To which Ch'en Sheng responded with the now-famous phrase, "The tiny birds do not know the mind of a hawk." Later, Ch'en Sheng raised an army of farmer-soldiers, rose in revolt, and destroyed the Ch'in dynasty.

🔺 🔺 🔺

To perform great achievements is the fundamental aim of the warrior, but what those achievements will be will depend on the kind of warrior. Up to now, your great achievements have been too rash. This is not what one likes in a military commander of the first order. Not taking into account the danger to yourself cannot be called an achievement.

At a certain battle during this time, daimyo Gamo Ujisato grappled with a strong opponent, and, at length, presented his severed head. Nobunaga, however, presented Ujisato, not with praise, but, after some moments, with the above words.

🔺 🔺 🔺

Finally, one of Nobunaga's most famous quotes sums up the life of this renowned warrior.

The courage a man has developed himself is superior to the courage with which he was born.

Takigawa Kazumasu
(1525–1586)

KAZUMASU SERVED as a general to Oda Nobunaga, who awarded him the governorship of Nagashima Castle in Ise for his meritorious deeds. He led the vanguard against daimyo Takeda Katsuyori in Nobunaga's Kai campaign, after which he became the governor-general of the Kanto region. After Nobunaga's death, Kazumasu joined forces with the general Shibata Katsuie, and fought against Nobunaga's general, Hideyoshi, but was defeated. He later fought as Hideyoshi's ally at Komaki and Nagakute, but was defeated by the forces of Tokugawa Ieyasu, who would later become the first shogun of the Edo period. In his later years, Kazumasu became a Buddhist monk, and died in the province of Echizen.

🔺　　　🔺　　　🔺

Try to understand my constant anxieties. Instead of envying the ever-vigilant cranes, you should enjoy yourselves like the happy little sparrows.

Takigawa Kazumasu once whispered this to a close associate. That day he was resting at a detached residence in the mountains, and at a slight distance could see a flock of wheeling cranes. The cranes, even when pecking at whatever they were feeding on, called out warnings in all directions, and never settled down. And though they were all of a kind, they remained scattered apart, and never came close to each other.

On the other hand, the numerous little sparrows gathered and played together on the branches of the garden plants and in the eaves, and even in the presence of human beings were unperturbed at their food. Kazumasu gave a sigh, and related the following to his friend.

It would be beneficial to compare those cranes with a flock of sparrows. The cranes are exactly like us. I have had good luck, and become a daimyo, received a large fief and a great number of men. But to say anything, I must think and then open my mouth; and if I want to eat, I'd better not do so without having someone test my food for poison. At night, there must be a wide-awake guard at my side, circling patrols outside, men to announce the hour, and they must be vigilant until I'm awake. My retainers, and even the people of my fief, look out for me day and night, and they can never pass a moment in pleasure.

This lays bare the difference in the lives of the daimyos of the Warring States period (1467–1615) and the daimyos of the following Edo period (1615–1868), a time of stability and peace. Indeed, it likely demonstrates the true feelings of those men at the top of the Warring States world. During this period of political and military chaos, a leader could not afford a single moment of negligence; and as administrators at the zenith of society, their lives were relatively miserable. More than anything, such an embrace of deep emotions may have meant failure for a man of military and political power. A man drawn to power could not afford any feeling that might lead to a state of relaxation.

In this connection, there were a number of examples of such feelings in China as well. Consider the following:

"Men understand the pleasure of fame and position, but do not understand the highest truth of the pleasure of being a nobody.

Men understand the misery of hunger and cold, but do not understand the extreme misery of being warm and well fed."

Ts'ai Ken T'an[1]

"The Master said, 'In late spring, people change into new clothes, groups of young people and their children will go down and bathe at the river, enjoy themselves in song, and return home.' The Master sighed and continued, 'I approve of such things.' "

Analects of Confucius

When Kazumasu spoke of the cranes and the sparrows, he was stationed at Umayabashi Castle in Kozuke Province and acting as the governor-general of the Kanto region. As the most powerful veteran general of the Oda clan, he had led the vanguard in Nobunaga's conquest of Kai Province, and utterly defeated the Takeda clan. Nobunaga had then placed him at Umayabashi Castle, and given him the responsibility for subjugating Kanto.

Only three months later, however, Kazumasu was informed of Nobunaga's death after an attack on the Honnoji temple in Kyoto. All of the military commanders who had only recently conquered the area now crowded at the castle gate, and he could not know what might happen if he announced Nobunaga's demise. And there was the matter of the Hojo clan, his powerful enemy in Odawara. Even a secret retreat to his home fief in Ise would

---

1. *Saikontan* (菜根譚) in Japanese. A book of wisdom written by the Chinese sage, Hung Ying-ming in the seventeenth century.

not likely go unchallenged, so perhaps it would be best to sally forth and strike first. Kazumasu gathered his generals together and began maneuvering, and it was at this point he unwittingly let slip the words that expressed his bitterness and anguish.

In the end, Kazumasu attacked the Hojo, but was beaten, and returned to Ise through Nagano along the Kiso Road. His former glory never returned, and he finally took the tonsure and led the rest of his life in seclusion.

Shibata Katsuie
(1530–1583)

AFTER INITIALLY PLOTTING against Oda Nobunaga, Katsuie submitted to the former and eventually became one of his most trusted generals. After his campaigns against Nobunaga's enemies, he was awarded with the fiefs of Echizen and Kaga, and married Nobunaga's sister. At the death of Nobunaga, he marched to attack the traitor, Akechi Mitsuhide, only to find that Hideyoshi had already defeated the man. His jealousy and resentment of Hideyoshi grew as Hideyoshi's star continued to rise, and the rivalry between the two ended with the siege of Katsuie's castle. Knowing that his cause was lost, Katsuie set fire to the castle, and died in the conflagration with his wife and servants. His wife's three daughters (by a former husband) were secretly led to safety, and the eldest eventually became Hideyoshi's mistress.

🔥   🔥   🔥

If the commanding general of the vanguard is not given authority and power, he will be unable to truly exert himself.

Katsuie was indeed ordered by Nobunaga to take the position of the vanguard's commanding general. When he strongly declined the position, Nobunaga was unrelenting, and after a prolonged argument, Katsuie gave in and withdrew. Later, in the environs of the castle, he chanced to bump into a samurai under Nobunaga's command, and when the man rudely accused him of being impolite, Katsuie cut him down.

When Nobunaga was informed of this incident, he became incensed, and commanded Katsuie to appear before him on the spot. When called to task, he responded, "Knowing that this kind of thing was liable to happen, I tried to decline my newly appointed position. Shall I now, without good reason, decline altogether? If the commanding general of the vanguard does not have authority, he is someone whose orders will not be obeyed."

Nobunaga had no response.

Akechi Mitsuhide
(1528–1582)

MITSUHIDE WAS ONE OF Nobunaga's ablest generals, and a culturally sensitive poet. He was first given the post of governor of Sakamoto Castle in Omi, and eventually given the fief of Tanba. Mitsuhide's eventual antipathy toward Nobunaga may have been caused by the latter's unjust public ridicule of him. In 1582, Nobunaga commanded Mitsuhide to lead a large number of troops to reinforce Hideyoshi's siege of the Mori clan. After a feint of starting out, however, Mitsuhide turned and attacked Nobunaga at the Honnoji temple in Kyoto, resulting in Nobunaga's suicide. When Hideyoshi was informed of this situation, he quickly made peace with the Mori and returned to Kyoto to attack Mitsuhide. In the confusion of events, Mitsuhide was killed by a mob of farmers, only thirteen days after he had declared himself shogun. Thus, he is known as the "Three Day Shogun."

🔺　　🔺　　🔺

When the Buddha tells a lie, it is called "skillful means";[1] when a warrior tells a lie, it is called "strategy."[2] Seeing this is so, one pities the common folk and farmers.

It is not clear when Mitshide made this statement, but what

---

1. Skillful Means (方便): an expedient way to teach the Buddhist dharma, designed to be in accord with the capacity of the hearer's understanding. This is the method of teaching in the *Lotus Sutra*.
2. Strategy (武略): this is based on Chinese strategist Sun Tzu's comment that "Warfare is the way of deception." (兵者詭道也).

is clear is that he was not an ordinary military commander. And, it is most ironic that he died at the hands of the very "common people and farmers" for whom he felt such sympathy.

🔺   🔺   🔺

The enemy is in the Honnoji.

With these words, recorded in the *Akechi gunki*, the chronicles of the Akechi clan, Mitsuhide turned his troops from their goal of aiding Hideyoshi in his campaign against the Mori, to attacking the unsuspecting Nobunaga who was resting at the Honnoji temple. They are now used colloquially by the Japanese when one's real intentions lie elsewhere than what is stated.

On June 1, 1582, Mitsuhide received Nobunaga's orders to decamp 10,700 troops to the Chugoku region. The *Akechi gunki* relates what follows:

"The forces were divided into three divisions: one was led by Akechi Sabanosuke, Shitennoji Tajima-no-kami, and Murakami Izumi-no-kami; another by Akechi Jiemon, Fujita Dengo and others; and the last by Mitsuhide himself, Akechi Jurozaemon, Araki Yamashiro, and Suwo Hida-no-kami. Leaving their quarters at Tamba Hotsu, they entered the mountains, and came out at Sagano in the province of Yamashiro. They then made camp next to the Jizo-in temple at the foot of Mount Kinugasa.

"Akechi Sabanosuke led his troops down the main road, passed the slope at Omi, and arrived at the village of Katsura in Yamashiro.

"Akechi Jiemon's troops went from the village of Oji in Tamba through the mountain paths in Karahitsugoe, and finally passed by the village of Yamada in Yamashiro.

"All of these armies urged their horses on through the night, and when they approached Kyoto, Mitsuhide made his official proclamation: 'Prepare your provisions, and set up your armor. The enemy is in the Honnoji in Nijo Castle, and we will attack and cut him down!'

"Both commanders and troops understood that this was treason, but called in their packhorses, gathered their military provisions, and began battle preparations. At length, they changed their route and proceeded toward the Honnoji."

There are no two gates to order and reverse;
The Great Way penetrates the source of the mind.
A dream lasting fifty-five years;
Awaking, I return to the Unity.

This is said to have been Mitsuhide's death poem.

After Nobunaga's death, Mitsuhide held supreme power for only eleven days. Hideyoshi, whose troops had surrounded Bitchu Takamatsu Castle for the campaign against the Mori, brought his forces back to Kyoto in a forced march in an astonishingly short time. The action at the Honnoji had taken place at dawn on June 2, and on the following day, Mitsuhide's messenger carrying a secret dispatch to the Mori, informing them of Nobunaga's death, was intercepted by Hideyoshi's men. On June 4, Hideyoshi made peace arrangements with the unsuspecting Mori, returned his troops to Kyoto, and encamped at Ozaki. On June 13, the twenty-six thousand warriors under Hideyoshi encountered the sixteen thousand men led by Mitsuhide on the banks of the Yodo River at Yamazaki. The battle lasted from late afternoon to nightfall.

Mitsuhide hoped to regroup, and headed back to his home base at Sakamoto. Midway, at a place called Ogurusu, the villagers there brought an end to his life of fifty-five years.

Hosokawa Yusai
(1534–1610)

BORN IN KYOTO THE SAME YEAR as Oda Nobunaga, Yusai—
whose given name was Fujitaka—was a close retainer of the
Ashikaga shogun, Yoshiteru. He later served Japan's three great
unifiers, Nobunaga, Hideyoshi and Ieyasu, and was highly re-
garded by all three. He was one of the few men who weathered
the chaos of the Warring States period relatively unscathed. Yusai had the reputation of being a sincere man who did not covet
power, and yet knew how to get along in the world. He had great
talent in political matters, but devoted himself to the arts of poetry and tea, at which he excelled. He was the author of no few
volumes. It is said that he laid the foundation for the system of
etiquette adopted by the Tokugawa shogunate.

🔺　　　🔺　　　🔺

**Learning is something that should be studied broadly. It is,
for example, like a beggar's bag in which he stores everything
from leftover meat to cold soup. After you have studied a
wide range of subjects and are well informed, you can listen
to an argument, and either take it or leave it.**

Yusai's studies ranged from poetry, to folklore, etiquette, tea
ceremony, classical literature and calligraphy; and he wrote on a
wide variety of subjects.

A number of Yusai's students and disciples became excellent
poets representative of the early Edo period. At the time of the

Battle of Sekigahara,[1] Yusai was at Tanabe Castle, under orders of Ieyasu's Eastern Army and, surrounded by Ishida Mitsunari's Western Army, was in difficult straits. The emperor Goyozei, however, was so concerned that the Way of Poetry would decline if Yusai were killed, that he brokered a negotiation of peace between the two parties.

Once, when he was still young, Yusai was in pursuit of an enemy general during a certain battle. Having lost sight of the man, he was ready to withdraw when one of his attending samurai pointed out the horse the general seemed to have abandoned and said, "Try to follow him just a little while longer." He then continued, "An old poem has it that 'My Lord seems to have not yet gone far; for the tears on his sleeves are not yet cold.' Look, the general's saddle is still warm, so I think that he must be nearby."

Yusai felt that this was probably true, and in the end, they were able to capture the enemy general. It was after this incident that Yusai began to take an interest in the Way of Poetry.

Though Yusai probably had the grounding in his later achievements at an early age, this story may well have been made up by someone at a later date. It does, however, express the fact that Yusai excelled at both the literary and the martial, and represented the epitome of the cultured warrior.

---

1. The Battle of Sekigahara took place on October 21, 1600, in what is now Gifu Prefecture, and was the deciding confrontation between the forces of Tokugawa Ieyasu and those loyal to Toyotomi family. Although the Tokugawa side was considered the "Eastern Army" and the Toyotomi the "Western Army" due to their headquarters in Edo and Kyoto respectively, warlords from all over Japan took sides with one or the other. The Tokugawa forces were victorious, and this ushered in a new era, the Edo period, that would last for some 250 years.

Maeda Toshiie
(1538–1599)

TOSHIIE FIRST SERVED ODA NOBUNAGA, but after the Battle of Shizugatake and the defeat of the forces of Shibata Katsuie, was attached to Toyotomi Hideyoshi and became the governor of Kanazawa Castle. In Hideyoshi's later years, Toshiie was appointed to be one of the five members of the Council of Elders, who would look after Hideyoshi's young son. Toshiie did his best to check Tokugawa Ieyasu's ambition to become shogun, but died only a year after Hideyoshi.

᛭ ᛭ ᛭

When you send a letter to someone of lower social standing than you, the more courtesy you use in the writing, the more grateful the recipient will be. If you think of the person as being an underling and write accordingly, it will be the same as stating the difference in rank quite clearly. This is something that foolish men of little character will enjoy.

Toshiie was once sent two carp by daimyo Fukushima Masanori. Toshiie then ordered his close retainer Emori Heizaemon to write a letter of thanks. Emori wrote, "We are satisfied with the arrival of the two carp." Toshiie told his retainer to rewrite the letter, and quoted the above to him.

᛭ ᛭ ᛭

When you go out onto the battlefield, you should act according to your own thoughts. It would be better not to listen to what someone else says.

When opposing forces on the battlefield are, perhaps, ten thousand men against three thousand, if the commanding general of the three thousand men uses his judgment, he may take the victory from time to time. This is because the men of the smaller force will fight with desperate determination. For this reason, the commanding general of a large force should not be negligent.

When attacking a castle, the man who impatiently dismounts too early and continues advancing on foot will invariably soon be out of breath. The skilled man will ride right up to the castle walls. Only in places where there is damp or swampy land should one act differently.

In his thoughts on battle, Toshiie may have been influenced by the *Wu Tzu*, a Chinese book on strategy, written by an author of the same name, who died c. 381 BC.

"One man thinking nothing of throwing away his life is enough to make a thousand men cower in fear."

Wu Tzu

* * *

The person with money will fear neither man nor the world at large. If he lacks finances altogether, however, he will fear the world and everyone in it.

* * *

It is not right to determine matters relying on the words of informants.[1] For if you have any favoritism toward the informant, you will begin to have doubts about your invaluable subordinates. This is damaging.

▲   ▲   ▲

You are but one of sixty-six men in Japan who hold a single province. You should be very mindful of this.

Toshiie's second son, Toshimasa, had been given the fief of Noto and was the governor of Nanao Castle with a stipend of 210,000 *koku*,[2] but seemed to have a penchant for enjoying himself. When, in 1596, the great Fushimi earthquake leveled his residence along with many others, Toshimasa quickly built a temporary "cottage,"[3] and invited his father over for a visit. As a post-earthquake "temporary cottage," it was a structure of some workmanship. Toshiie silently received his son's hospitality, but on his return, sent a messenger back with the above words, indicating that he advocated modesty and frugality, regardless of a powerful position.

▲   ▲   ▲

---

1. Informant (横目): lit. "side-glance." During the Muromachi period (1333–1573), there was often an official who inspected the activities and behavior of the daimyo's retainers, and would issue secret reports on their results. Toshiie forbade this practice.
2. *Koku*: the measure of rice determined for a man's stipend. One koku was approximately five bushels of rice. While a daimyo like Toshimasa would receive a stipend of 210,000 koku, for example, a single swordsman like Miyamoto Musashi received only 200.
3. Cottage (小屋): this word literally means "hut," "hovel," or "cottage," but can also mean "theater" or "playhouse," and this secondary meaning may give a hint of what Toshimasa's structure was like.

The Kanpaku[4] is not a man of real aspirations. His rebellion was clearly a sham. If we have hopes for our own descendants, we should not involve them in such luxuries.

Before his own child was born, Hideyoshi had adopted his nephew, Hidetsugu, and ceded to him the title of Kanpaku. But when his son, Hideyori was born, Hideyoshi's attitude toward his nephew deteriorated. Finally, in 1595, Hideyoshi banished Hidetsugu to Mount Takano, and forced him to commit suicide. The reason for this was said to be that Hidetsugu had made plans for a rebellion. At length, more than thirty people, including Hidetsugu's children, wife and concubines, were executed on the riverbed at Sanjo in Kyoto. The daimyos—including powerful warlord Date Masamune—who had been intimate with Hidetsugu were reprimanded, and his family doctor and poetry teacher were exiled.

Hidetsugu's confiscated mansion was given to Maeda Toshiie. When Toshiie received this reward, he proceeded with an inspection of the place, and was shocked at its magnificence. Having a part of it torn down, he said the above words.

---

4. Kanpaku: the title held by Hideyoshi's nephew, Hidetsugu. It was the most powerful office of that time, and was, in name, chief advisor to the emperor.

Yamanaka Shikanosuke
(1545?–1578)

A POPULAR HERO, Shikanosuke served the Amako clan, which dominated the San'in area. He was considered the first of the so-called "Ten Brave Samurai of the Amako."[1] After the Amako were crushed by daimyo Mori Motonari, Shikanosuke made great efforts in 1568 to reinstate clan member Amako Katsuhisa as a power in the area. Katsuhisa regained authority for some time, taking charge of Kozuke Castle, but in 1578, was attacked by Mori clan members Kikkawa Motoharu and Kobayakawa Takakage, and committed suicide inside the ramparts.

🔺　　🔺　　🔺

Having a great military advantage is not enough; you must simply be determined to die.

This is Chinese strategist Sun Tzu's "Law of the Jaws of Death." When a man has no place to run, he will fight desperately, and likely live to fight again.

If you surround an army, be sure to leave them an opening [for escape]. A desperate army should not be pursued.
The Art of War VII/36

---

1. The ten brave retainers who attempted to reinstate the Amako clan after its decline that began in 1566. The clan was completely destroyed in 1578.

Give me seven hardships and eight afflictions.

Shikanosuke always prayed to the gods in this manner. When someone asked why, he responded:

If you don't test yourself when encountering difficulties, you'll never know the extent of your own abilities.

Hori Hidemasa
(1553–1590)

HIDEMASA FIRST SERVED Oda Nobunaga as the governor of Nagahama Castle in Omi. After the Honnoji incident, in which Nobunaga lost his life after an attack by Akechi Mitsuhide on the Honnoji temple, Hidemasa followed Hideyoshi, orchestrating the fall of Akechi Mitsuhide's Sakamoto Castle. Eventually he became the governor of Sawayama Castle in Omi. Hidemasa pacified the northern territories, and was enfeoffed at Kitanosho Castle in Echizen. In battle at Odawara, he led the vanguard, but later became sick and died at Shinagawa in the province of Musashi. It is said that Hideyoshi mourned his death with great lamentation.

🔱　　🔱　　🔱

Many different kinds of people will receive stipends from the clan of a daimyo.

There was a certain man, a retainer, who was always going around with a tear-stained face. He had a poor reputation among the clan's members at large, and the chief retainers finally advised Hidemasa to relieve the man of his duties. Hidemasa replied, "Is there anyone better suited than this man as a messenger for memorial services and funerals? We find work for many different kinds of people in the clan of a daimyo."

🔱　　🔱　　🔱

When it comes to things one needs, the loss of ten sheets of gold leaf is not particularly regrettable. But as far as useless things go, you should not waste a single sheet of paper.

After rewarding someone with ten sheets of gold leaf, Hidemasa smoothed the wrinkles out of ten sheets of bundled paper, and put them in a box. He was resolved to use them when he had to, but, as he told his close retainers in an on-the-spot lesson, "Useless things are never really so."

⚜   ⚜   ⚜

Isn't there anyone here who will remonstrate with me like this? This is a matchless gift from Heaven. The placard upon which this was written is our clan's treasure.

Once, Hidemasa secretly went down to the town around the castle, and set up a placard criticizing his own governing practices. His chief retainers had no idea that he had done this, and when they became aware of the sign, they were shocked, and advised him to search for the criminal and give him a severe punishment. At length, Hidemasa read the placard carefully, adjusted his *hakama*,[1] rinsed his mouth, bowed to the placard three times, and spoke the above words to his retainers.

---

1. *Hakama*: a man's formal pleated pant-skirt.

Toyotomi Hideyoshi
(1536–1598)

HIDEYOSHI WAS BORN the son of a farmer–foot soldier from the village of Nakamura in the province of Owari. At the age of twenty-two, he began to serve Oda Nobunaga. At thirty-one, the story has it that he built a castle overnight at Sunomata, an act for which his wit and resources are still celebrated; and at thirty-eight, he led the vanguard in the attacks on the Asai and Asakura clans, and was made the governor of Otani Castle. At the age of forty, Hideyoshi defeated daimyo Takeda Katsuyori at Nagashino, and at forty-two, set out for the campaign in the Chugoku region. At age forty-seven, while still in Chugoku, he was informed about the Honnoji incident in which Nobunaga lost his life, immediately returned to the capital, and defeated Akechi Mitsuhide, who had brought about Nobunaga's death. At forty-eight, he destroyed the forces of the general Shibata Katsuie; and at forty-nine, fought and then made peace with Tokugawa Ieyasu. At fifty, Hideyoshi became Kanpaku [chief advisor to the emperor] and took the surname Toyotomi. At the age of fifty-two, he subjugated the island of Shikoku, and at fifty-five, attacked Odawara and destroyed the Hojo clan. His son Hideyori was born a year after Hideyoshi embarked on his first invasion of Korea at the age of fifty-seven. He passed away at the age of sixty-three.

🔱   🔱   🔱

Oda Nobunaga was a brave general, but not a particularly good one. He only knew that the hard can win over the soft, but did not know that the soft can subjugate the hard. Once he had acted upon someone with hostility, the other's resentment did melt away to the very end, and it was as though he had cut away at the roots and withered all the leaves. Thus, he punished those who had submitted, killed those who had surrendered, and there was no end to his enemies. This was due to the narrowness of his magnanimity and a lack of caliber. Though people showed him respect, they had no love for him. For example, if someone thought he was going to be bitten by a tiger or a wolf, he would kill the animal to escape danger. This is what gave birth to Akechi Mitsuhide's rebellion.

Hideyoshi was just the opposite of Nobunaga in this regard. He did destroy his enemies, but those who surrendered were received in the manner of hereditary vassals, and treated with magnanimity.

Date Masamune, one of the most powerful warlords of this period, had expressed hostility toward Hideyoshi, but, realizing Hideyoshi was on the rise, reluctantly joined in the siege of Odawara. But when Masamune entered Hideyoshi's camp, he was given the latter's own sword to wear with the words, "Go out and strike them down."

This is one reason why Hideyoshi was able to unite the country. Two years after his death, at the Battle of Sekigahara,[1] there were not a few of his close allies who joined the forces of his long-time enemy Tokugawa Ieyasu. The battle, however, was not truly between the Toyotomi and the Tokugawa, but between Ishida Mitsunari, one of Hideyoshi's most loyal generals, and Tokugawa Ieyasu, and Ieyasu had cleverly brought many generals who had antipathy toward Mitsunari to his own side. Nevertheless, Ieyasu had to wait for sixteen years after Hideyoshi's death before he could directly confront the Toyotomi clan as an enemy.

---

1. See note, page 78.

As for a master, he may employ a man for a year, and if he finds the man to be of no use, may dismiss him. As for a retainer, he may work for a master for three years, and if he finds the master to be unfitting, may take his leave.

There are many daimyo and commanding generals who left precepts from the standpoint of hiring others, but very few who made statements from the standpoint of the person being hired. Hideyoshi, who began his career as a foot soldier, was unique in this regard. He is supposed to have said this upon leaving the service of Matsushita Yukitsuna, his first master.

In battle, a 60 to 70 percent win is sufficient. If you continue to beat on the vanquished unmercifully, they may feel that there is no way to escape, and become resolved. Thus they may become much stronger than they originally were. In the strategy for attacking a castle, you attack at one point quite clearly, but let the enemy know that there is a route of escape. In this way, you will quickly gain the victory.

In April of 1578, Hideyoshi received orders from Oda Nobunaga to attack the province of Harima, and so surrounded Noguchi Castle. Those under the command of the governor of the castle put up a stiff resistance, but were unable to withstand the attack, and sued for peace. Hideyoshi's retainers said, "If they were this way before we fought them, what can they do now?" and advocated annihilating those in the castle altogether. Hideyoshi restrained them, and advised them with the above.

Hideyoshi often used this way of thinking, with the result

that few people were sacrificed, and the strategy brought excellent results.

✻   ✻   ✻

No matter where you go, if you do not find it satisfactory, you should return home. They will embrace you any time.

Hideyoshi made this statement when he was still a subordinate officer. If any of the clan retainers desired to take their leave, he would summon them, make tea for them himself, and present them with a short sword. Then, when they came back to him, he would greet them with good grace.

✻   ✻   ✻

To hoard great quantities of silver and gold would be the same as keeping a good warrior in jail.

Hideyoshi's generosity is acknowledged by the historical record. Every time he stepped out, he took along a large purse of money, and would give cash to children who were just passing by or to beggars on the road.

✻   ✻   ✻

Since I have taken the entire country, no matter how much I have given to the daimyos, their provinces are all mine. So if the land taxes do not go into my own store houses, it still amounts to being sustained by a meal a day from these men.

Hideyoshi was quick to assign fiefs to the various daimyo. And not just bit by bit, but in a rough and ready way of entire provinces or even two. The above words were his response to his close retainers when they worried about a loss of land taxes. But as he eventually gave out too many fiefs, there were, in the end, none left to award his vassals, and instead, he gave out famous swords made by Masamune.[2] Still, there were only a certain number of these swords in existence, and the great number of counterfeit Masamunes found today are said to be the result of Hideyoshi's over-generosity.

Although I now rule the entire nation, I do so without ever having cut a man down with my sword. By my influence, however, I have had others do the cutting, and with such judiciousness, I regulate the land.

When Yagyu Munenori—who would later become sword master to both Tokugawa Hidetada and Iemitsu—was young, he was once beckoned to the presence of Hideyoshi's son and heir, Hidetsugu. Hidetsugu had heard that Munenori was famous for being able to take an opponent's sword with his bare hands, and wanted to see this once for himself.

When Hidetsugu unsheathed his sword and made a pass at Munenori, the latter made a quick move, and kicked the young man. The sword left Hidetsugu's hand, and landed about thirty feet away.

Munenori immediately bowed low with his head to the floor, saying that he had meant no disrespect, but kept his eyes quite open. Hidetsugu, however, was extremely impressed. Exclaiming,

---

2. Masamune (1264–1343): one of the greatest sword makers in Japanese history. A number of his descendants took his name, and the swords that were made by some of the members of his school became equally coveted items.

"This was just as I expected! You've performed splendidly!" he became Munenori's disciple.

Hidetsugu later summoned retainer Kinoshita Hansuke and, in front of his father, Hideyoshi, announced Munenori's abilities, and recommended him highly. Hansuke replied, "Hidetsugu, were you really able to do something like that?"

When Hansuke said this, Hideyoshi immediately fell into a bad mood and said, "Doing such things, you'll never be able to follow in my footsteps. While you have the status for ruling the nation, you learn useless techniques like taking someone's sword away bare-handed. A commanding general doesn't do stupid things like that."

Truly angered, he spit out the above quote concerning sword and politics.

⚜   ⚜   ⚜

> **Deep in the mountains,**
> **stepping over autumn leaves,**
> **the chirping of fireflies.**

Hideyoshi's artless style seems to have been considerable. A review of the historical facts and countless anecdotes demonstrate unmistakably how he must have made a strong impression upon the people of his time. The tale about this rather curious haiku is typical.

A famous *renga*[3] poet was naturally exasperated when he saw this poem. When he said quite seriously, "A firefly is not an insect that chirps," Hideyoshi calmly responded, "Even if a firefly has no voice, if I think it does, it's going to have to chirp."

This story may be fiction, but it is derived from the fact that

---

3. *Renga*: linked verse.

Hideyoshi was not particular about fine details. The following is another.

Hideyoshi was having someone write the Chinese characters "Daigo" (醍醐)[4] in front of him, but the man could not remember how to write the character *dai*. Hideyoshi saw that the calligrapher was confused, and drew another, simpler character with the reading *dai* (大) with his finger on the straw mat floor and said, "If you don't know [the right one], this one will do."

"Great undertakings do not rely on fine details."
                                    Records of the Grand Historian

＊   ＊   ＊

You should not drink too much sake. You should not sleep too late in the morning. You should not become bored with things. Use discrimination for even the smallest of affairs. Find pleasure in pain. Find pain in pleasure. Be moderate in matters of physical desire. Be wise about what will happen after your death. Leaders of men should be verified. You should not engage in horseplay. Stay out of the way of drunks.

＊   ＊   ＊

When selfishness enters into the relations between lord and vassal, or between friends, discord is the result. The things that I like may not be those that others enjoy. And it is the same with retainers: there are many things they find unpleasant. Commanding officers should pay attention to this as well. Select close retainers that are much like you, and secretly put your own watchdog into place. Then, from time to

---

4. Daigo (885–930): the 60th emperor of Japan.

time, receive his opinions, listen to what he has to say about
your own good and bad points, and pay attention to everything around you. This is the first important business of a
commanding general. If you are not informed of such things,
you will never know your own mistakes, your faults will gradually increase, you will become estranged from others, your
clan will fall, and you will only cause damage to yourself.

In his later years, at least before Hideyori was born, Hideyoshi was not a conventional dictator. In one view, he was
unbridled and licentious, but he made meticulous plans, and,
especially in terms of human relationships, was careful to watch
himself with a sharp objectivity. He placed people to be his own
mirrors, and sought out their opinions.

Generally, when people are facing death they will leave their
final testament; but when very ill, because their consciousness my be clouded, they can say nothing. I am not going to
do this. I will leave my will while I am tranquil and without
problems.

Hideyoshi's final words are said to be the following:

When you are correct, you may first be weak, but will later
be strong. When you are perverse, you will at first look good,
but will later surely cause damage.

In April of 1598, Hideyoshi hosted a huge flower-viewing
party at the Daigo-ji temple. In July, his health took a turn for
the worse, and by August, he had made all the daimyo swear allegiance to his son Hideyori. On September 5, thirteen days before

he died, he entrusted Hideyori's future to the so-called Council of Elders: Tokugawa Ieyasu, Maeda Toshiie, Mori Terumoto, Uesugi Kagekatsu and Ukita Hideie. It is said that he passed away in peace, assured that these men would care for his son, and so establish his line for generations. It was the height of autumn, and Hideyoshi was sixty-three years old.

His death poem:

> As the dew falls,
> As the dew fades away,
> So does my life.
> All I achieved at Naniwa:[5]
> A dream within a dream.

---

5. Naniwa: Osaka. Referring to the huge castle and castle town he had established there.

Takenaka Hanbei
(1544–1579)

HANBEI WAS Toyotomi Hideyoshi's chief military strategist. A man of gentle looks, it is recorded that he had the "appearance of a young lady." There was nothing rough about him at all, but the way he thought and acted was courageous and resolute. For this alone he was respected by others. He was first a vassal of the Saito clan, but deserted warlord Tatsuoki, attached himself to Nobunaga, and then served Hideyoshi. Many of Hideyoshi's victories were owed to Hanbei. When he died of a disease contracted at the front, Hideyoshi's grief was immeasurable.

🔺　　🔺　　🔺

When people ask about battle, they do not inquire about the essentials as they should. By concluding their interviews without asking about such things, nothing is accomplished. Those who answer are also like this. In the end, there are an extraordinary number of conversations that amount to nothing.

🔺　　🔺　　🔺

Since ancient times it has been natural that a samurai would wear his sword at his side, even in a room. Recently, however, the sword is removed and placed elsewhere, and may be put with many others. A man of proper intentions should have some understanding concerning this. If many swords are put in the same place, a man is liable to grab the wrong one if there is an emergency. Thus, if another man lays his sword

on its side, you should place yours in an upright position, or in some opposing way, or in another place altogether.

There was a story circulated that Hanbei gave instructions on the battlefield riding around on an ox. There was no seeming reason why he should be mounted on an ox, but it probably indicates his imperturbability. His calm demeanor and meticulous care can be seen in this way of placing swords as well.

🔆　　　🔆　　　🔆

You should have the understanding that as soon as you step out from under the eaves of your house, the enemy is there waiting for you. It would be extreme carelessness for you to step over this line inattentively.

In his later years, Hanbei practiced extreme caution when going outside. No matter how much Hideyoshi depended on him, he continued to be vigilant and no doubt had the foresight that he might become estranged from his superior at some point. Or, it may have been a sort of camouflage to keep Hideyoshi reassured.

🔆　　　🔆　　　🔆

You should not buy a horse for a price that exceeds your station in life.

Hanbei advised, "If you intended to buy a horse for ten *ryo*, be restrained enough to buy one for five. If you have to dismount and abandon it, you will know that with the remaining five ryo, you may buy another. Thus, you will have no attachments."

Gamo Ujisato
(1556–1595)

UJISATO WAS A SON OF Gamo Katahide, the governor of Hino Castle in Omi. When he was young, Ujisato was held as a hostage[1] by Oda Nobunaga, but as he got older, he followed Hideyoshi, and at the age of twenty-one, became the governor of Ise Matsushima Castle. He was initially deeply trusted by Hideyoshi, and after the destruction of the Hojo clan at Odawara, was made the governor of Kurokawa Castle in Aizu, to check the power of warlord Date Masamune. Ujisato restored the castle, renamed it Wakamatsu Castle, and made it his base of operations. Due to the local lacquerware industry, the castle town attracted many artisans and prospered. Ujisato died of an illness at the age of forty, en route to Kyushu to participate in Hideyoshi's invasion of Korea.

🌲   🌲   🌲

Matsukura Kensuke was brave and decisive, and with great ambitions. He was not a man satisfied to be in a subordinate position. Therefore I promoted him quickly. If I had protracted his advancement a little, however, he would not have been uselessly struck down and killed. It is my own fault that I have lost an excellent warrior.

---

1. Hostage (人質): powerful daimyo often demanded hostages from the families of lesser powers to insure their loyalty. Such "hostages" were treated well, however, and, according to their rank, often in the role of honored guests. Ujisato, for example, was later given Nobunaga's daughter in marriage.

Matsukura Kensuke was a ronin who sought an official position under Ujisato. He had originally been a vassal of daimyo Tsutsui Junkei, but because of some untoward incident had been labeled a coward, and left the Tsutsui clan altogether. Ujisato was impressed by the man's forthrightness, thought that he had promise, and enlisted him into his ranks. Not long after, there was a battle, and Kensuke performed feats that made him stand out from the crowd. Ujisato promoted him to the rank of captain, and rewarded him with a stipend of 2,000 *koku*.

Kensuke felt a strong sense of gratitude, and at the next battle rushed unreasonably deep into the enemy lines, and was struck down and killed, Ujisato grieved for Kensuke, and spoke the above words to his close retainers.

This anecdote is sometimes interpreted as a indication of Ujisato's compassion and human-heartedness, but this may be a superficial understanding. Ujisato was by no means a run-of-the-mill warrior. At the time of the first invasion of Hideyoshi's Korean campaign,[2] Ujisato had decamped from his faraway new post at Aizu and was marching toward Kyushu. On the way, he passed by his old hometown in Omi, and wrote,

> How deep in my thoughts:
> > The way we come and go
> Is never really set.
> > My old home town
> > I would see as a passerby.

Ujisato was a unique warrior, and it was a shame that he died in the prime of life.

---

2. The Korean campaign is a broad term for Toyotomi Hideyoshi's two invasions of Korea, the first in 1592, the second in 1597. Both invasions ended in the defeat of the Japanese forces.

Ujisato's feelings about Kensuke bring to mind the ancient Chinese Taoist text, the *Chuang Tzu*, which he had undoubtedly read. In this book are the lines:

"The twisted and bent tree cannot be used in any way. Therefore it has attained a fine old age."

The twisted and bent tree cannot be used as lumber, so is left to stand. But the straight tree can be used for lumber and is quickly cut down. Thus the useless live long lives, and the useful are cut down early.

🔺　　🔺　　🔺

These days, some clan traditions emphasize harmony, and value kindness and mercy. Thus, many of their samurai are soft and weak. Too many are moved by righteousness, and have deep understandings of etiquette, and too few have courage and daring. On the other hand, there are some clan traditions that are too strictly martial. Many of their samurai are deeply mindful of the Way of the Warrior and quite strong, but there are few who are moved by righteousness or who understand etiquette. Both such clans are lacking. To illustrate, in spring and summer all things in nature grow and develop, but there are many people who fall sick at such times, things easily rot, and worms and maggots abound. This is like placing too much value on kindness and mercy. Fall and winter are seasons when the trees and foliage wither and decline, and yet many things ripen and mature at such times. For these reasons, a clan should not have traditions that are too tight and strict. A commanding general of true caliber will keep his clan's traditions correct, so that they will not lean too much toward spring, summer, fall or winter.

When leading troops as a commanding general on the battle field, if you only yell, "Charge! Charge!" there will be some that will do no charging at all. But at the point of ordering men into combat, if the general will himself lead the charge, and yell, "This way!" no one will abandon him. If a general thinks that he can send his men into a charge while he himself stays behind, there will be no charging whatsoever.

After Ujisato's first military action at the age of fourteen, he participated in a number of battles, including those at Komaki and Nagakute. Among these, however, it was at the siege of Iwaishi Castle during Hideyoshi's campaign against the Shimazu clan in 1587, where he won fame for his courage. Just when the enemy's resistance had become vehement, and the attacking troops were becoming disheartened, Ujisato rushed out to the very front, dashed into the thick of it, and brought on the surrender of the castle.

In the end, however, it was not simply a matter of taking the lead; but of having the men respond to their various duties. When Ujisato himself dashed out in front of all the others, it was a moment when his men were faltering, and the attack stagnating; and his aim was to transform the moment into an opportunity to strike.

Listen, those people who are labeled "wise men" generally have knowing looks, speak cleverly, and cloud the eyes of others with their talents and learning.

This was Ujisato's assessment of a man by the name of Tamagawa Soma. Tamagawa was a man who spoke elegantly with great erudition, and was judged as being extremely able. When someone recommended him to Ujisato, the latter was delighted, beckoned him to his presence, and treated him as a guest of honor. The two talked every night for ten days, discussing various subjects, but then Ujisato gave him some money and sent him away. The man who had made the recommendation, thought for sure that Ujisato would employ Tamagawa, and so was quite disappointed; and even Ujisato's close retainers thought this dismissal to be rather strange. Ujisato responded to their dismay with these words: "Tamagawa praised me, but spoke ill of all the other daimyo, and talked on and on about his own many personal contacts. Sooner or later, he will be employed by some daimyo, who will be happy for a while with a new talented vassal. But after a while, this man will begin to wield power over others, will avoid the elder retainers, and will be the cause of internal disputes. People will then change their minds, and actually admire this insight."

A   A   A

Retainers should be treated with deep affection, and be awarded with fiefs. If a daimyo has no affection for his retainers, but only gives out fiefs, the situation will not go well. On the other hand, if he has affection for his retainers, but awards no fiefs, the affection will be in vain. Fiefs and affection are like the two wheels of a cart, or the two wings of a bird.

Ishida Mitsunari
(1560–1600)

MITSUNARI ENTERED THE service of Toyotomi Hideyoshi at the age of thirteen, and performed meritorious services in the area of administration. He became the governor of Sawayama Castle in Omi, and later participated in Hideyoshi's invasion of Korea as a member of staff of its commanding general, Ukita Hideie. After the death of Hideyoshi, he resisted the rise of Tokugawa Ieyasu, and created an alliance of the daimyo in the Kansai region. His forces were defeated at the Battle of Sekigahara on October 21, 1600.[1] Edo-period historians have depicted Mitsunari as somewhat of a villain, but this is, perhaps, a case of history being written by the victorious. The truth would seem to be that he was a man of character and talent. He had, indeed, been selected by Hideyoshi as one of the five commissioners administering the country, and was given the responsibility for the city of Sakai, the important and wealthy port city adjacent to Osaka. He is said to have descended from the aristocratic Fujiwara clan.

🔺　　　🔺　　　🔺

That's poisonous to the phlegm. I won't eat it.

Mitsunari was captured seven days after his defeat at Sekigahara, while hiding out at Mount Hibuki and trying to plan a comeback. He was taken back to Kyoto, paraded around the city, and executed at the bank of the Kamo River in the area of

---

1. See note, page 78.

Rokujo. Before his execution, Mitsunari asked for hot water to quench his thirst. His guard said that he had no hot water, but offered him some dried persimmons. When Mitsunari refused the fruit with the above quote, someone nearby laughed, noting that Mitsunari was just about to be executed. The condemned man replied, "I can imagine you all might think that way, but a man who understands a just and righteous cause will take care of his life right until the moment his head is cut off. Such is the man who would accomplish his aim no matter what happens."

It is said that Mitsunari met his death at the river bank calmly, with no change in his complexion.

🔺   🔺   🔺

Dogs and cats have the tiger's stripes, but the reason people do not consider them valuable is because they are not tigers at all. When someone has a degree of wisdom and uses it as an ornament, people are liable to misjudge the dog or cat for the tiger.

🔺   🔺   🔺

When a servant receives an allowance from his master, he should use it entirely, so that nothing remains. To have something remain is theft. But only a fool would spend too much and then borrow money.

Fukushima Masanori
(1561–1624)

MASANORI AT FIRST SERVED under Hideyoshi, and after the Battle of Shizugatake in 1583 was the first on the list of the "Seven Spears."[1] After distinguished service in both the attack on Odawara and the Korean campaign, he was granted Kiyosu Castle in Owari Province, with a stipend of 240,000 *koku*. After Hideyoshi's death, he opposed the forces of military commander Ishida Mitsunari, and joined Ieyasu's forces at the Battle of Sekigahara.[2] For this he was awarded Hiroshima Castle and a stipend of 490,000 koku. In 1619, he fell out of favor with the shogunate, and was removed to Kawanakajima in Shinano Province, with a stipend of only 45,000 koku. There he became ill and died at the age of sixty-four.

🔺　　　🔺　　　🔺

Look at the bow. During hostilities you should regard it as an important treasure. During times of peace, it is slipped into a bag and put in the warehouse. I am such a bow: used in times of conflict, but now in times of peace, put into this warehouse of Kawanakajima.

🔺　　　🔺　　　🔺

---

1. The title given to the seven men who performed the most courageous feats with spears.
2. See note, page 78.

"People's minds are turning for the worse." This has been said every generation since ancient times. If this were true, it should be quite apparent today. But if this is not true, it is only a conjecture.

Masanori's opinion is echoed in the writings of Machiavelli:

"People praise the past, and speak ill of the present. The reason for this is that they neither understand the past nor have any direct connections to it."

Discourses on Livy

Before military action on the field commences, the disposition of men cannot be regulated. And even if it is, the hot-blooded one will dash out to the front, while the timid will stay to the rear. Some in the rear will go to the fore; some in the fore will fade to the rear.

This was Masanori's response to being asked about the placement of men just before the beginning of a battle. He knew that a commander could not expect a set formation, but would have to "organize" in response to changes on the field. Thus, the way of battle is not fixed, but adapts to situations as they arise.

Kato Kiyomasa
(1562–1611)

KIYOMASA WAS BORN in Nakamura in Owari Province, the same village as Hideyoshi, to whom he was related. From his youth, he served under Hideyoshi, and at the Battle of Shizugatake was numbered among the "Seven Spears."[1] For his record of active service and his meritorious deeds on the battlefield, he was awarded half of the province of Higo. Decamping for the Korean campaign, he led the vanguard troops, but during the campaign opposed Ishida Mitsunari and temporarily incurred Hideyoshi's displeasure. At the Battle of Sekigahara,[2] he allied himself with Ieyasu's Eastern Army, as a result of which he was awarded Higo Kumamoto Castle, with a stipend of 540,000 *koku*. Kiyomasa invested great effort into harmonious negotiations between Hideyori and Ieyasu, but died while the process was still ongoing. Three years later, Ieyasu commenced the attack on Osaka Castle that would lead to Hideyori's death and the end of Hideyoshi's line.

🔥　　🔥　　🔥

It is said that those below follow the example of those above. Thus, if a commanding general relaxes even for a moment, those below him will become greatly negligent. The mind of one man at the top will permeate ten thousand men beneath him.

🔥　　🔥　　🔥

1. The title given to the seven men who performed the most courageous feats with spears.
2. See note, page 78.

When you use a person, do so according to his capacities.

Kiyomasa led the vanguard troops in Korea, and spent, in all, seven years on the Korean peninsula. Once, his troops were fighting in the vicinity of Pusan. As evening came they were in the difficult position of having to withdraw a company of men from a salient position. Kiyomasa looked around to see whom he might order to take charge of communications and backup, and decided upon Shobayashi Hayato, one of the lowest-ranking vassals among them. As ordered, Hayato was able to fulfill his responsibility, withdrew the troops without incident, and returned to camp.

At that time, however, one of Kiyomasa's retainers by the name of Morimoto Gidayu shed bitter tears. When Kiyomasa wondered what was wrong and asked the man about this, the latter responded, "I'm mortified that although I was right here next to you, I did not receive that order."

Kiyomasa laughed and said, "With your character, you would have fought with outrageous energy, and would have sacrificed a great number of men. There is a place for your kind of action, but in this case I thought Shobayashi was best fitted for the situation."

⚜ ⚜ ⚜

**Articles with which All should be Resolved,
Regardless of High or Low Rank.**

- **A retainer should not be careless in the way of service. He should rise at four in the morning, train in the martial arts, eat his meal, practice archery, marksmanship, and horseback riding. A well-trained warrior should become more so.**
- **When a samurai goes out for amusement, it should be with such out-of-doors activities as hawking, hunting deer, and sumo wrestling.**

- When it comes to clothing, something within the range of cotton and raw silk will be fine. A man who wastes money on clothing and brings his household finances to extremities is out of order. Customarily, a man should prepare himself with the appropriate armor, support his retainers, and use his resources when there is some military action.

- When keeping company with other retainers, a man should limit the meeting to one guest and one host. The meal should consist of simple brown rice. When practicing the martial arts, however, he may associate with many people.

- As for etiquette and decorum during military action, a man should remember that he is a samurai. A man who is fond of unnecessary embellishments is out of order.

- Practicing arts such as dancing and the like is strictly forbidden. When you take up the sword, it must be for the purpose of cutting a man down. Everything comes from where you place your concentration of mind. Therefore, people who practice dance, which is not connected to the martial arts, should be ordered to commit seppuku.

- A samurai should be assiduous in matters of Learning. He should read military books, and exert himself exclusively in the virtues of loyalty and filial piety. Reading Chinese poetry, linked verse and traditional Japanese poetry is forbidden. If a man becomes acquainted with such extravagant, graceful and elegant things, he will become just like a woman. He has been born into the house of a warrior, and thus his intentions should be firmly set in the way of dying while grasping the long and short swords. If a man does not inquire constantly into the meaning of Bushido, it will be difficult for him to die an honorable death. For this reason, it is essential to keep the mind in great military spirits at all times.

- A samurai should observe the above articles night and day. If there is anyone who finds it difficult to be equal to these articles, he should be given his leave, an investigation should be carried out immediately, it should be officially noted that he was unable to follow the Way of Man, and he should be driven out. This has been stated as it is beyond any doubt.

By 1603, the country had at long last been unified, and Kiyomasa had become the governor of Kumamoto, but a number of traditions and customs of the Warring States period remained. The following is a story about how Kiyomasa was bested by his pages in this regard.

One day, Kiyomasa was to hold a tea ceremony, and had his most famous tea bowl taken out for the occasion. Unfortunately, one of his pages accidentally broke the precious bowl. The pages talked over the situation together, and decided that they would not tell Kiyomasa the name of the boy who had broken the utensil; if there was to be a punishment, they would all be punished together.

Kiyomasa was unaware of their resolve, and when he inquired about who the guilty person was, no one would say a word.

"You cowards!" Kiyomasa yelled angrily. "All of you are staining the names of your fathers, who have been praised so highly for their brave martial deeds!"

At that point, Kato Heizaburo, a fourteen-year-old youth, said, "We made a pledge not to divulge the name of who this might be, so you wouldn't be able to condemn him to death. What's more, there's no reason for you to go so far as to refer to our fathers' brave deeds on the battlefield in this matter."

"What an insolent brat!" Kiyomasa mumbled, and got up and left. But despite the sour look on his face, it was clearly understood that he was pleased at how the young boys had matured.

Kato Yoshiaki
(1563–1631)

YOSHIAKI SERVED HIDEYOSHI, and was declared one of the "Seven Spears"[1] at the Battle of Shizugatake. Later, he became the governor of Masaki Castle in Iyo. During the Korean campaign, he took an active part in naval operations, and made a name for himself by capturing a number of ships. He opposed Ishida Mitsunari, and joined the Eastern Army of the Tokugawa forces at both the Battle of Sekigahara[2] and the siege of Osaka Castle. When the grandsons of daimyo Gamo Ujisato died without heirs bringing about the extinction of the Gamo clan, Yoshiaki was enfeoffed at Aizu. He is said to have been a man of prudence and deep deliberation.

⚜   ⚜   ⚜

Yoshiaki was a careful and meticulous man. In his clan, it was forbidden for a man to tie his sash[3] at his back; rather it was to be tied at the front and to the side. In a moment of emergency, a sash's knot easily came undone, and if tied at the back, it could not quickly be re-tied. Another consideration was that if a man had to run, a sash tied at the front and to the side could be adjusted without the man having to stop.

---

1. The title given to the seven men who performed the most courageous feats with spears.
2. See note, page 78.
3. During this period, a man's sash was worn outside of his garment. His sword's scabbard was held tightly inside of the sash.

Throughout Yoshiaki's mansion, there were folding screens painted with illustrations of generals' armor and helmets. For even if you knew the armor of a particular general, it might be hard to recognize it amid the confusion of battle. So the paintings were executed in detail with brilliant colors and the names of the various generals were also brushed in. These were placed in the long corridors for the benefit of everyone's thorough knowledge.

When a general changed his armor, or altered it with repairs or mending, an artist was quickly called in to make the proper adjustments to the paintings. It goes without saying that this practice was quite valuable when the men were engaged in battle.

A man of courage and ardor may perform deeds enough to make others open their eyes in surprise, but thorough and securely executed military exploits will be performed by a man of integrity, simplicity and loyalty.

If a man constantly thinks that he is inept, he will make no blunders. The man who acts with a show of being clever, will invariably make mistakes.

You should take great care with the workmanship of your helmet. If the worst happens, and your head is taken by the enemy, your helmet will accompany your head when it is placed

before the opposing general. The rest of your armor can be shabby. It will just be thrown aside somewhere anyway.

🔺　　　🔺　　　🔺

It is said that "Virtue and human-heartedness are to be considered treasures, while money and jewels are not," but this is a saying for kings, princes and generals. For people like us, it's better to say that "Good men are to be considered treasures, and so are silver and gold."

This would seem to be typical of Yoshiaki, who managed to survive the turbulent years of the Warring States period, when others did not. After leading his troops on a forced march from the island of Shikoku to the site of the Battle of Sekigahara, he noted that "If I had not put away plenty of gold and silver, I would have been unable to move."

Nabeshima Naoshige
(1538–1618)

NAOSHIGE WAS THE FIRST DAIMYO of the Saga Nabeshima clan. A relative by marriage to the Ryuzoji clan, who first governed the area, he was a counselor to daimyo Ryuzoji Takanobu, and, with a long record of active service, eventually took the real control of the fief. After Takanobu's death, he received the governorship of Saga Castle and a stipend of 350,000 *koku*. In close contact with Ieyasu, he acted in concert with the Eastern Army, and attacked the castles held by generals of the Western Army during the Battle of Sekigahara.[1] Many of his sayings and deeds are recorded in the book *Hagakure*.

🔥　　　🔥　　　🔥

No matter whether a clan be of high or low status, when the time comes, it will collapse. If it resists the collapse at that time, the collapse itself will be unseemly. But if it is recognized that the time has come, the clan will fall with grace.

🔥　　　🔥　　　🔥

To keep a watchful eye over a man who does not warrant such is foolish. But not to do so over a man who should be watched is foolish as well. It is of utmost importance to know how to look at men.

🔥　　　🔥　　　🔥

---

1. See note, page 78.

It is a fundamental principle that when a man has something to say, he should delay opening his mouth for a little while; but when he has firmly settled something in his mind, he should do it right away.

🔥   🔥   🔥

No matter how wise another man may be, you should not depend on him, but rather, understand you are on your own.

🔥   🔥   🔥

You should not spend too much time ruminating on momentous events. In all things, if you ponder them for too long, nine out of ten will turn out for the worse. A warrior is someone who is quick, rough and ready.

🔥   🔥   🔥

Among men, there are three ways of thinking. The best is when a man recognizes another's conduct to be discerning, and makes it his own. The middle level is when a man hears an opinion contrary to his, and makes it his own. The worst is when a man is told good information and just laughs at it.

🔥   🔥   🔥

There are three kinds of men's wisdom. The best is when a man hears something good, masters it himself, and puts it into action. The middle level is when a man hears something good, but never really learns it; and even if he learns it, it never occurs to him again. The worst is when a man hears something good, and it goes in on ear and out the other.

115

Gather a number of good men around you, and have them impart their wisdom or speak of their concerns. Making their thoughts your own is of first importance.

Things that are unpleasant to me will be to my benefit.

It is difficult to know what lies in the future. Simply stay deeply concerned, and you will know what lies ahead.

A castle can be or not be beneficial. For the good general who has good men, a castle will be useful. For the inferior general who employs inferior men, a castle will have no use, regardless of how secure it may be.

When a battle is won, the awarding of stipends is of good use; but when a battle is lost, a stipend awarded without a word of compassion will have no benefit at all.

Be resolved that, in battle, you do not fall into the enemy's expectations.

✲ ✲ ✲

Whatever gives you a nice sensation at the time will surely be a cause of regret later on.

✲ ✲ ✲

Draw out what your subordinates have to say, and listen to them well. It is common knowledge that gold lies underground.

✲ ✲ ✲

Even those people you find unpleasant should be drawn into your presence. You will invariably gain from this practice.

✲ ✲ ✲

Know pain and exertion as much as those in the lower classes do.

Tokugawa Ieyasu
(1542–1616)

BORN AS THE ELDEST SON of the governor of Okazaki Castle in the province of Mikawa, at age six, Tokugawa Ieyasu became a hostage[1] of Oda Nobuhide. From age eight to age fifteen, he became a hostage of daimyo Imagawa Yoshimoto. When Yoshimoto was killed at the Battle of Okehazama, Ieyasu—nineteen years old at the time—was freed from his ties to the Imagawa, and returned to his home province. At the age of twenty-one, Ieyasu entered into a defensive and offensive alliance with Nobunaga, and eight years later united with the later and defeated the alliance of the Asai and Asakura clans on the northeastern shore of Lake Biwa. In 1572, when Ieyasu was thirty-one, he was attacked and defeated by Takeda Shingen, who was marching toward the capital of Kyoto; but only three years later defeated the army of the head of the Takeda clan, Takeda Katsuyori at the Battle of Nagashino. At the age of thirty-eight, in order to keep the support of Nobunaga, he killed his wife (who had been a member of the Imagawa clan) and forced his eldest son to commit suicide. In 1582, Nobunaga killed himself after the attack on the Honnoji temple in Kyoto. Ieyasu hastened to Kyoto with his troops, but returned to Okazaki when he heard of the death of Akechi Mitsuhide (whose victory at the temple had brought about Nobunaga's suicide) and Hideyoshi's ascendancy. Two years later, the combined forces of Ieyasu and daimyo Oda Nobuo were defeated at Komaki.

---

1. Hostage (人質): powerful daimyo often demanded hostages from the families of lesser powers to insure their loyalty. Such "hostages" were treated well, however, and, according to their rank, often in the role of honored guests.

By the age of forty-five, Ieyasu had become a titular vassal of Hideyoshi, but in another twelve years, Hideyoshi passed away. In 1600, Ieyasu's Eastern Army defeated the Western Army of Ishida Mitsunari at the Battle of Sekigahara,[2] and at the age of sixty-two, Ieyasu received the title of Sei-i Taishogun. When he turned sixty-four, Ieyasu entrusted his son Hidetada with the office of shogun, and ten years later destroyed the remnants of the Toyotomi clan at the siege of Osaka Castle. Ieyasu died the following year at the age of seventy-five.

＊   ＊   ＊

"What if the cuckoo won't sing?"
Nobunaga: "I'll kill it."
Hideyoshi: "I'll make it sing."
Ieyasu: "I'll wait for it to sing."

＊   ＊   ＊

A clever man is not a man with great wisdom.

When Ieyasu was young, and being held as a hostage by the Oda clan, he was once offered the gift of a mockingbird.[3] His retainers thought this was a novel curiosity, but the young Ieyasu[4] refused to take the bird, and returned it to its owner. When asked why, Ieyasu replied, "That bird probably has no voice of its own. It's the same with human beings—the man who is clever in some little way will not have great wisdom. A commanding general will not fool around with a man who has no wisdom of his own."

---

2. See note, page 78.
3. Mockingbird (物真似鳥). Probably not a mockingbird, which does not live in Japan, but more likely a mynah or crow.
4. Ieyasu's name at this time was Takechiyo.

🔺   🔺   🔺

Those who brought the Heike down to defeat were the Heike. Those who destroyed the men at Kamakura, were the men at Kamakura.[5]

Ieyasu believed that the Heike clan were not destroyed by exterior enemies. The cause of their destruction was within. Carelessness, luxury, a lack of harmony, backstabbing . . . all of these were carried out among themselves.

🔺   🔺   🔺

The proper way of holding a besieged castle is the following: strengthen the gate, position your archers and gunners, draw the enemy as far as the bridge in front of the gate as if everything was going according to their plan, and then suddenly release your arrows and bullets. When you have carefully observed the state of confusion in the enemy's ranks, dash out of the gate and strike. If you easily take charge of the situation at top speed, the castle will be held in fine fashion. But if you think that you must hold the castle at all costs, draw up the bridge, and cower within, your soldiers will be unable to brandish their strength, and in the end, the castle will fall.

---

5. The Heike clan had grasped full control of the government in Kyoto by 1159. They became arrogant, aped the aristocracy and grew slack in their martial practices and responsibilities. Their rule came to an end in 1185, after which they were supplanted by the Genji (or Minamoto) clan, who then established the Kamakura in shogunate 1192. The city was reduced to ashes in 1333 during the Genko war, and the Genji fell for many of the same reasons attributed to the fall of the Heike.

To Ieyasu, the bridge was not something to let the enemy cross over, but was rather an apparatus for his own troops to cross. Even when you are defending a place, you do not lose the initiative. This is the posture of active defense. Ieyasu spent many years in the field, and while it may appear from the outside that he took a passive attitude, he eventually held the nation in the palm of his hand. This tactic may have been one of the secrets to his success.

Another successful tactic may have been his skillful use of men. In 1591, the Kunohe Rebellion broke out in Mutsu Province. The year before, Ieyasu, who had just been given command of the castle at Edo, was appointed by Hideyoshi as commander-in-chief for subjugating the area. Ieyasu himself went on horseback to order Ii Naomasa, the governor of the domain of Ueno Minowa—a stipend of 220,000 *koku*—to depart for the front. Someone offered his opinion to Ieyasu, and said, "Rather than dispatching a man of such high rank, wouldn't it be better to first send someone of lower status? Then, if that were not successful, you could send Naomasa." Ieyasu responded, "If I first dispatched a man of a more humble position, and the matter was not settled, then I would have to send a man of higher rank. In that case, the first man would lose face, and have no other choice than to die in battle. Rather than uselessly kill off my vassals, it's far better to be careful from the very first, and be doubly sure."

⚜   ⚜   ⚜

The death of an enemy general like Shingen is absolutely nothing to rejoice in.

In 1573, Ieyasu's powerful enemy Takeda Shingen became sick and died. At the time, Shingen held the provinces of Kai, Suruga and Shinano, had made alliances with the shogun Ashikaga Yoshiaki in Kyoto and daimyo Asakura Yoshiaki in Echizen Province, and was on his way to make a pincer attack on Nobunaga in the provinces of Owari and Mino. He had already invaded the domain of Ieyasu, Nobunaga's ally, and Ieyasu had suffered a great defeat at Mikatagahara the year before. It was thought to be a matter of time before Shingen's great army overcame the alliance of Nobunaga and Ieyasu, advanced to Kyoto, and took over the entire country. Incredibly, Shingen passed away at that very moment.

Needless to say, there was great rejoicing in the barracks of Nobunaga's and Ieyasu's men. And certainly Shingen was an old enemy who had caused Ieyasu great difficulties for many years. But Ieyasu reproved his subordinates with the following words: "Thanks to this powerful enemy Shingen, we have braced ourselves for a great task, we have organized our military preparations, and striven to improve our statecraft. The death of such an enemy general is absolutely nothing to rejoice in."

In the end, after the destruction of the Takeda clan, Ieyasu instructed his subordinates to collect the instruction books and weapons from the period when Shingen flourished, and had the old retainers of the Takeda tell him about Shingen's doings. He made a detailed study of these things, and made his former enemy's strategies, tactics and administrative methods his own.

🔻   🔻   🔻

In a place where you think there may be the slightest danger, dismount from your horse.

It is said that Ieyasu, from the time he was young into his old age, would deliberately get off of his horse and walk in dangerous places. It is recorded that, in order to be thoroughly careful and to keep the horses in good condition, Ieyasu would tell his close retainers that this was a secret principle of the Otsubo school.[6]

🔺　　🔺　　🔺

Hiking your robe up above your buttocks when crossing a river that only comes up to your knees may seem to be a little too cautious, but you won't have the problem of getting wet.

🔺　　🔺　　🔺

Men of lower rank have the advantage of cultivating and improving themselves together with friends. In this way, it is easy for them to understand their own mistakes.

Men of higher rank are different, and do not have the benefit of mixing with friends, and so improving themselves. Thus, they do not know when they have gone too far.

🔺　　🔺　　🔺

When there are a number of fellow cowards, they will cover for each other. Their own actions will be talked up by their fellows, and they will speak up for them in return. Thus, they rejoice in themselves, and envy those who are better than them. These are the traits of great cowards.

🔺　　🔺　　🔺

Generally speaking, in both ancient and modern times men in high positions who will not listen to admonishment lose their provinces and destroy their clans.

---

6. Otsubo school: the school of horsemanship established by Ozuka Ya-suhide in the fifteenth century.

Ieyasu would listen attentively to his subordinates' opinions whether they were worth taking or not. He once said to one of his close retainers, "If a man's advice is useful, I'll put it to use. If it isn't, I won't. But I respect the frame of mind in which an opinion is given."

🔺　　🔺　　🔺

A chief retainer who sees the wrongdoing of his master, and criticizes him, is far and away of a better mind than the man who charges out as the first man on the field of battle.

It is more difficult to criticize one's lord than to be the first man out on the battlefield. Ieyasu commented on this fact: "Certainly a man puts his life on the line if he rushes out to be the first on the battlefield. But victory or defeat depends on fate, and even if he dies, he will be lauded by his master, and leave fame to his descendants. It is understood in advance that there is no loss whether he lives or dies. The man who criticizes his master, however, will find victory precarious eight or nine times out of ten, and may even suffer death or house imprisonment."

The difficulty of reprimanding a lord was touched upon by the ancient Chinese philosopher Han Fei Tzu, and the words "incurring imperial wrath" (逆鱗にふれる)[7] come from a section of his eponymous book, the *Han Fei Tzu*, covering this subject:

"The trick of giving advice is neither in the art of speaking nor in some special knowhow. Rather, it is in reading the mind of the person to whom you will speak, and in adjusting your opinion appropriately."

---

7. 逆鱗 (*gekirin*): literally, opposite scales. This is "rubbing a person the wrong way."

The dragon is a good-tempered animal, but beneath its throat are scales that grow in the opposite direction of the others. If you touch these scales, you will be bitten and killed. A ruler also has these opposite scales. If you are able to make proposals without touching them, you are an excellent man."

★　　　★　　　★

To disregard a person's talents, and to value him according to his rank or stipend, is not the way to use a man.

Once Ieyasu appointed retainer Takagi Kiyohide to be a messenger, and appointed Kakei Masashige, a man of a lesser stipend, to the higher office of administrator in charge of banners and pennants. When one of Ieyasu's close retainers expressed surprise at this, the former replied, "I think that each person has an appropriate responsibility, and appoint them accordingly. If Masashige's stipend is too low, perhaps we should increase it."

★　　　★　　　★

Generally speaking, it is an absolute necessity for a lord to distinguish between a man's correctness and incorrectness. A man may put on a good appearance, but if he is not well liked and the people do not obey him, he is likely nothing but a scoundrel.

★　　　★　　　★

In employing a person, a good general will engage him for his strong points. It's just like a good doctor and his use of medicine. He knows what will be efficacious and what won't

be, and makes his prescription accordingly. In this way, he treats the disease skillfully. A mediocre doctor will not know whether a medical treatment is efficacious or not, and will make his prescription arbitrarily. This can be the cause of a patient's death.

In the same vein, Ieyasu once said, "When you employ a man, it is imperative that you seize upon his strong points. It's like your ears, eyes, mouth and nose. Each one is useful for what it administers. A cormorant is able to dive under the water; a hawk is able to fly high in the sky. Each and every person has his strong points. Do not demand that a man do any job whatsoever."

⚜   ⚜   ⚜

Water will float a boat, but it will also cover it completely.

Ieyasu instructed his son Hidetada on this matter, comparing a lord to a boat, and the lord's chief retainers to the water, echoing the words of Confucian philosopher Hsun Tzu, in his book of the same name:

"The lord is a boat, the people are the water. Thus, the water can float the boat, or cover it completely."

⚜   ⚜   ⚜

A bright lord or a good general will harvest the good things others have done, and so regulate the province.

Ieyasu taught that one should imitate the good things others have done without hesitation. At the time of his campaign into Mutsu, he saw the remains of a placard that shogun Minamoto no Yoritomo had erected nearly four hundred years before, and it made a deep impression on him. The placard had been erected after Yoritomo had defeated ruler of the northern provinces Fujiwara no Yasuhira and subjugated his territory. On it was written, "I will follow the policies of Hidehira [Yasuhira's father]." Because of this, Yoritomo's rule was peacefully secured.

When Ieyasu occupied Kai Province, he imitated the practices of the Takeda clan; and when he took the Kanto region, he practiced the policies of the Hojo clan.

⚜　　⚜　　⚜

There are three ways of governing a province. The first is called managing the province, the second is called managing the people, and the third is called managing provisions. Governing the province with a good understanding of its size, topography, cultivated areas, mountains and fields, and rivers and sea coasts is called managing the province. Governing the province by managing the disparity of the population, and by not being confused by production is called managing the people. Governing the province by managing its abundance or poverty is called managing provisions.

Historically, many of the provincial lords made the claim that their governmental policies were based on a system of morality and ethics. In contrast, Ieyasu said the way of governing a province was through management. Management, then, he saw as the calibration of efficiency.

⚜　　⚜　　⚜

For someone with low status like me, rare curiosities do harm, and are absolutely of no benefit. All in all, if you have

a fondness for rare articles, they dwindle your resources, and in the end, you'll have nothing with which to take care of your samurai.

When Ieyasu was still a subordinate to Nobunaga, he received, at the beginning of one November, the gift of a splendid peach tree. Everyone thought it was wonderful and praised it highly, but Ieyasu would not take it. When someone thought this was strange, and asked Ieyasu about this, he laughed and uttered the above words.

When a man is looked upon well by his lord, he becomes prideful without being aware of it. This is human nature, and there is nothing new about it. But when a man's pride knows no bounds, and he is unaware of it altogether, it will be very quickly noticed by others.

After Ieyasu withdrew from his position, and was living in Suruga Province, he was once visited by an envoy from his son, Hidetada. Noticing that this envoy was favored by his son, Ieyasu admonished the man with the above words.

The vassals who are the ministers of state should be in harmony. If something happens and the shrubs catch on fire, the entire mountain can burn down. When the administrative vassals contend, the province can collapse.

The failures of Nobunaga and Hideyoshi were in large part due to the failure of the policies of their top vassals. Ieyasu's successes, it can be said, were largely due to the policy successes of his own top vassals.

❧   ❧   ❧

There is nothing outstanding about being militarily prepared during times of conflict. This is just like a mouse biting a man when in the throes of being caught. Being prepared during times of peace, however, is the sign of a man who truly loves the martial.

This calls to mind a similar quote from the ancient Chinese text the *I Ching*:

"The Gentleman[8] does not forget the dangerous when he is safe; does not forget death while he is alive; and does not forget disturbances when the country is in order. In this way, his position will be secure, and the state will be maintained."

❧   ❧   ❧

It is a serious malady to want to appear somewhere, to cut a fine figure, and to accomplish everything on your own. People who think in such a way, no matter how bright and full of knowledge they may be, and no matter how well they bring things to a conclusion on a certain instance, will surely fail sooner or later. Theirs is a talent that is of no use.

❧   ❧   ❧

---

8. The Gentleman (君子): the Confucian ideal.

Regardless of the matter, first make your decrees strict; if you then gradually make them more lenient, the people will still be respectful of the public law, and make no transgressions. In this way, there will naturally be no criminal cases. But if at first you are lenient, and become strict later on, you will have death penalties beyond your expectations for people you would rather not kill.

The man who would be a commanding general will never defeat the enemy if he only sees the backs[9] of his troops.

While it is true that a man who serves a lord should not be addicted to bribes, if one is too scrupulous, the people of the province will not feel that they can approach or be friendly with him. In this way, he will never know their good or evil doings.

From the very dawn of the New Year, you should be mindful of the coming New Year's Eve.

---

9. Backs: literally 盆の窪, the nape of the neck. In other words, the commanding general should be leading his troops, not encouraging them from behind.

Honda Tadakatsu
(1548–1610)

TADAKATSU SERVED IEYASU, and helped in the latter's campaign to unify the nation. So impressed was Ieyasu with Tadakatsu's courage and talents, that he referred to him as one of his *Shitenno*, or the Four Great Kings of Heaven,[1] the others being Sakai Tadatsugu, Sakakibara Yasumasa, and Ii Naomasa. Six years younger than Ieyasu, he stayed constantly at his lord's side protecting him from danger, and cut his way through tough situations a number of times. Hideyoshi was also favorably disposed toward Tadakatsu, and hoped to win him over to his own camp, but Tadakatsu was loyal to Ieyasu to the very end. Famous as a fighter, he participated in fifty-some battles. After the Battle of Sekigahara,[2] he was enfeoffed at the domain of Kuwana in Ise Province with a stipend of 150,000 *koku*.

🔺   🔺   🔺

The mind is easily influenced by the physical world.

Tadakatsu clearly understood the reality that, though a man might be a warrior, his mind could still be moved by a stipend or fief. He was known to place inordinate importance on the control of the will.

---

1. The Four Great Kings of Heaven: 四天王. The four gods of heaven, each guarding one of the four cardinal points.
2. See note, page 78.

Tadakatsu was popular as a warrior of positive qualities. It was said that "There are two things that surpass Ieyasu: a Chinese helmet and Honda Tadakatsu." At Tadakatsu's death, a man by the name of Otani Sanpei committed *junshi*.[3] In turn, one of Otani's retainer's committed junshi to follow *him* in death, leaving this poem:

> Accompanying him in death,
>> Ahh, accompanying him in death.
> Yet, for all that,
>> How I rue my lord's affection.

---

3. *Junshi* (殉死): committing suicide (usually by seppuku) to accompany a lord in death.

Honda Shigetsugu
(1530–1596)

SHIGETSUGU WAS ONE of he three commissioners of Mikawa Province. He fought for the Tokugawa clan in a number of their battles, including Nagashino, Komaki and Nagakute, and was known as *Oni Sakuza*—the Demon Sakuza—for his ferocity in battle and his forceful personality. He lost both an eye and a leg from battle wounds.

Shigetsugu was known as strict but fair when it came to the rule of law, and wrote out those laws in the simple *kana* syllabary so all could read them. He was enfeoffed with a stipend of 3,000 *koku* in Kazusa Province by Ieyasu, but died before the latter became shogun.

It is said that Shigetsugu was a man of few words, who was simple in nature and liked clarity.

✩   ✩   ✩

To write simply: be careful with fire, do not let Osen get thin, And fatten the horses.

This was sent to his wife while traveling, and is famous as an example of the simplicity of his writing. Osen was Shigetsugu's child. Another version goes, "Simply and respectfully, be careful with fire, do not make Osen cry, and fatten the horses."

Honda Masanobu
(1538–1616)

FROM THE LOW POSITION of falconer, Masanobu became one of Ieyasu's trusted strategists. He was enfeoffed at Tamanawa Castle in Sagami with a stipend of 22,000 *koku*, and refused to take any increase. It was Masanobu's son, Masayoshi who devised the tactic of filling in the moats at Osaka Castle after the winter campaign,[1] enabling the castle to be more easily approached. Masanobu died two months after Ieyasu, aged seventy-nine.

🔥   🔥   🔥

You may understand avoiding harm, but not understand the harm in avoiding harm. Once you have shrunk back from another's power, you may not be able to straighten up again.

Two year's after Hideyoshi's death, Ieyasu defeated Ishida Mitsunari at the Battle of Sekigahara,[2] and assumed hegemony over the entire nation. But recent conditions in the country had become complicated, and one wrong move would have turned all the efforts he had made until now into bubbles floating downstream. Before Hideyoshi passed away, he had appointed a Council of Elders (consisting of Tokugawa Ieyasu, Maeda Toshiie, Mori Terumoto, Uesugi Kagekatsu and Ukita Hideie), as well as Five Administrators (Ishida Mitsunari, Nagatsuka Masaie, Soda

---

1. Ieyasu's attack on Toyotomi Hideyori, ending in January 1615, and resuming as the summer campaign the following May.
2. See note, page 78.

Nagamori, Asano Nagamasa and Maeda Gen'i) to guarantee the power of the Toyotomi line. Ieyasu was the most powerful of these men, but the others, aligned with the Toyotomi, were also strong and influential, and it was impossible to tell which way other warlords might go if there was a conflict among them.

Seven months after Hideyoshi's death in August 1598, his friend Maeda Toshiie, who had been specially appointed to protect Hideyoshi's son, became ill and died. This was Ieyasu's big chance: some counseled him that this was an opportunity to defeat Toshiie's son, Toshinaga. Ieyasu summoned Masanobu for his advice. The latter's counsel was, "If you act hurriedly, you will lose popular favor. You should try to win the Maeda clan over."

In the end, the antagonism between Ieyasu and Ishida Mitsunari (a strong supporter of Hideyoshi's son) came to a head. A rumor was spread that Mitsunari was going to rupture the dikes of the Yodo River, and flood Ieyasu's mansion, and Ieyasu was advised to evacuate.[3] Again, Ieyasu sought Masanobu's opinion. In a reverse approach from his former judgment, Masanobu advocated taking a positive countermeasure toward Mitsunari, and spoke the above words, which are famous in Japan. His meaning was that if Ieyasu avoided Mitsunari's aggressiveness now, all the commanding generals who were watching the situation and playing wait and see, would join the latter's cause. It goes without saying that the end result was exactly as Masanobu had forecast.

🔺 🔺 🔺

Doing construction in the winter that ought to be done in the summer will only wear out the workers, and it's more

---

3. Evacuate: 避難, literally "to avoid trouble." In the above quote, "avoiding harm" is 避害; essentially the same meaning.

labor than is necessary. Anybody knows when it's time to cut lumber or bamboo.

Masanobu was known for his practical outlook. Once, Ieyasu launched a frugality campaign, and put Masanobu in charge. At New Year's, Masanobu put up the customary pine and bamboo decorations over his gate, but on a much larger scale than in previous years. And, for the first Noh chanting on January 3, he erected a much larger candle than usual. Ieyasu thought this strange, considering the frugality campaign, but when he asked Masanobu about it, the latter replied, "I've been living economically for some time now just so I could do this."

🔥   🔥   🔥

My lord has thought to honor me for my humble services; but I request that he not increase the stipend of my son, Masazumi, after I am gone.

Masanobu said to Masazumi: "I am sure that you will be given an increase [in stipend] after I pass away. My services have been equal to a stipend of 30,000 *koku*, and for you to receive this much will be fine. But for you to accept more than that would bring disaster." Masanobu understood that too much advancement in the world could be dangerous. After he died, Masazumi became a member of the shogun's Council of Elders. In 1619, he was enfeoffed at Utsunomiya with a stipend of 150,000 koku. Three years later, however, he incurred the antipathy of the retainers of Hidetada (Ieyasu's third son, who would become the second Tokugawa shogun), was exiled to the far northern province of Dewa, and died of an illness there. It is said that the people at that time wondered at Masanobu's prescience.

Itakura Katsushige
(1545–1624)

KATSUSHIGE LIVED AS A monk until the age of forty. Thereafter, he served Ieyasu, by whom he was greatly valued. He was appointed magistrate of Suruga, and then of Edo, and finally Deputy of Kyoto, an office he occupied for twenty years. When the country was united by the Tokugawa shogun in 1603, and the country's seat of power moved to Edo, Katsushige suppressed any remaining influence of the Toyotomi clan in Kyoto, and made great efforts to win over the sentiments of the people. In 1620, Katsushige's son, Shigemune, succeeded to the office of deputy, while Katsushige became the governor of Iga.

⚜   ⚜   ⚜

I am not equal to this responsibility. I should go home, consult with my wife, and then give you my answer.

This was Katsushige's response when Ieyasu appointed him to the office of magistrate of Suruga. It was almost unthinkable that a man would say something like that at that time, and even today he might be considered henpecked. And, when Katsushige arrived home and informed his wife of the matter, she was shocked and said, "If this were some private matter, I could understand, but why are you asking me about something official like this?" To which Katsushige replied, "Since ancient times, there have been countless examples of men who held responsible positions, who not only fell in status, but lost their homes as well. They have committed losses of impartiality either because of their relatives or because they accepted bribes. And the causes of such things have often arisen from women. If I were to accept this office, will I not hear complaints from you about the requests of your relatives? Do you have enough self-confidence not to receive their gifts? And will you not meddle, no matter what I do, and no matter what kind of strange situation[1] I get myself into?"

At that moment, Katsushige's wife pointed out that his *hakama*[2] was twisted in back. Katsushige began to take off his hakama. "Didn't I just say that you shouldn't meddle no matter what kind of situation I was in? With this sort of behavior, I cannot take this office!"

His wife became flustered and apologized. In one of the records of the time, it was noted, "His wife was greatly shocked, repented, and wrote a number of 'admissions of neglect,'" or, in other words, written apologies.

In the end, Katsushige assented, went to Edo Castle, and told Ieyasu that both he and his wife had thought the matter over deeply, and that he would accept the position.

🔺   🔺   🔺

Ruling the country is like putting miso into a square container, and taking it out with a round ladle.

When Ikeda Mitsumasa, the fourteen-year-old daimyo of Bizen was returning from a visit to Edo, he passed through Kyoto and visited Katsushige, who was acting as Deputy at that time. When the boy asked for his advice as to how a province should be ruled, Katsushige replied with the above quote, meaning that

---

1. Situation: the word here is 身, which could refer either to Katsushige's body or his status, and by implication, a situation.
2. *Hakama*: a man's formal pleated pant-skirt.

you shouldn't be too exacting: you won't get everything out of the container, so don't try. Although Mitsumasa was young, he was highly praised for his intellect and ability, and Katsushige's words hit the mark.

The most important point about being a magistrate, is not taking bribes from the townspeople. If you are firm about this one thing, you will be able to make clear judgments.

When Ieyasu appointed a certain Hikosaka Mitsumasa to the office of magistrate, Mitsumasa firmly declined, pleading that he was not mature enough for the position. Ieyasu advised the man to go talk to Katsushige for advice. When he asked for instruction, Katsushige responded with the above words.

Kuroda Josui
(1546–1604)

KURODA JOSUI WAS BORN in Himeji (with the given name Yoshi-taka), and served Nobunaga. When military commander Araki Murashige rebelled against the latter, Josui was sent to dissuade Murashige from his course of action, but was imprisoned. He later took part in Hideyoshi's campaigns, in central Japan, at Odawara and in Korea. Along with Takenaka Hambei, he was considered one of Hideyoshi's greatest strategists and was granted a large fief in Kyushu. When suspected by Hideyoshi of further ambitions, retired and took the name Josui. During the Battle of Sekigahara,[1] he fought against the Western Army in Kyushu, thus securing his clan's fief. Although Ieyasu attempted to reward him with an office in the new government, Josui declined, and continued in retirement in Kyushu. He had been baptized a Christian and remained faithful to Christianity to the end of his life.

⚜   ⚜   ⚜

Generally speaking, there are people with whom you get along well, and those with whom you do not. This is especially true when a lord takes a retainer into service. Though there are a great number of retainers, there are always some who catch the lord's fancy. If such retainers are good men, the fief will be like a precious jewel; if they are bad men, they will obstruct its well-being. Thus, one should consider this carefully.

As you all know, among the warriors there are some with

---

1. See note, page 78.

whom I get along with quite well, keeping them close at hand and giving them light employment. However, I am resolved not to be infatuated by such men. As I am likely to be partial to them and to overlook their wrongdoings, I would ask you to please be on the lookout, and admonish me when necessary.

Well then, you, too, are likely not immune to taking the wrong measures with those with whom you get along well, and those with whom you do not. To those with whom you get along well, you are likely to think that their bad deeds are good, or you may be deluded about corruption. Knowing these things not to be good, you remain on intimate terms. Those with whom you do not get along well, however, you consider bad men even when they are good; and even when they are reasonable, you think of them as otherwise. Thus, each of you should be mindful about your compatibility with others, and how you deal with them.

When taking on a warrior, the very first thing is how you engage him. I finally understood this after the age of thirty, and everyone should take this to heart. A brazier is useless in the summer, but is necessary in the winter; an umbrella is useless on a sunny day, but is necessary when it rains. Meditate on this well; if you are impatient, a warrior will not serve you well.

If a great general does not have dignity, it will be difficult to command ten thousand men. However, if you misunderstand this and purposefully display an intimidating authority, you will cause yourself great harm.

If a job is not fitting for a retainer, there will soon be some fault. But if you think this through, the assignment of the work was an oversight on the part of the lord. Rather than blame the retainer, the lord should feel shame.

You should fear the punishment of your lord more than punishment from the gods. More than the punishment of your lord, you should fear punishment from your retainers and the common folk. The reason for this is that by prayer, you may avoid the punishment of the gods; and by apologizing, you may receive your lord's pardon. But if you neglect your retainers and the common folk, neither prayer nor apology will effect a pardon. Indeed, you will lose your domain. This is most fearful of all.

During the Battle of Sekigahara, the Kuroda clan had sided with the Eastern Army, had achieved meritorious deeds and had been enfeoffed in Chikuzen. Josui had already retired, but moved with his son Nagamasa to their new domain. They very quickly made repairs on edifices like the Tenmangu and Hokozaki shrines in Dazaifu. Josui was also a Christian at that time, baptized with the name Don Simeon, and, after the death of the Christian daimyo Konishi Yukinaga, protected the missionaries. He was famous for making the above statement.

Whoever aims to take the country should not think about either parent or child.

In the Battle of Sekigahara, both Josui and his son Nagamasa fought as allies of the Eastern Army. Josui was at Nakatsu Castle in Kyushu and, at the request of the Eastern Army, joined in battle with Otomo clan leader, Yoshimune, eventually capturing the castles at Aki and Kokura. Nagamasa followed Ieyasu directly and attacked the castle at Gifu, surrounded Kobayakawa Hideaki,[2] forcing the latter to change sides and thereby greatly helping to bring about the defeat of the Western Army.

Nevertheless, it is said that Josui's heart was elsewhere. Which is to say that if the action at Sekigahara turned into an extended battle and its outcome not determined, he was resolved to stay in Kyushu, becoming yet a third force in the conflict, with the goal of taking hold of the entire country. Years later, when Josui was on his deathbed, he told Nagamasa about his resolution at that time and confessed that he was willing to take the gamble even if it had resulted in Nagamasa's death, hence the above words.

🜸   🜸   🜸

Generally speaking, people have their own strengths and weaknesses. For myself, from the time I was young, when I took up the spear or the sword and confronted an opponent in single combat, I was not very skillful. In attacking one or two thousand of the enemy, however, I am quite accomplished.

🜸   🜸   🜸

To love specializing in the martial arts and to be a man of rash courage is the accomplishment of the lower class of warrior; it is not the way of a great general. Again, personally

---

2. Some sources have him as Hideyoshi's adopted son. He was actually the nephew of Hideyoshi's wife.

handling the spear, the sword, the bow and the horse—all the martial arts—are practices for the lower ranks; yet, if a general does not practice them as well, it will be difficult for the rank and file to improve themselves. Grasping the foundation of things, the general should himself practice the martial arts *and* study the finer arts such as poetry or calligraphy, thus leading all warriors to advance.

Whether of high or low rank, you should be resolved to carry yourself appropriately and to live within your means. There should be no negligence in this. Arrange the construction of your house, your clothing and all your furnishings slightly lower than your estate. It is essential that you use good judgment and not neglect your inherited duties. In the same way, your regular meals should be light and you should not take a trivial liking for elegant cuisine. As for having immoderate weapons made with ornate fittings, such are all the acts of people of fame. Such fame, however, is close to the foundation of financial problems.

One day a retainer with a stipend of 1,000 *koku* came to pay his respects to Josui and brought him a small gift of vegetables. Josui was very pleased and praised the man's thrift. Two or three days later, a man with a stipend of 700 koku visited him with a gift of two liters of sake. Josui received this with gratitude.

Four or five days later, a man with a stipend of only 100 koku came by and presented Josui with a sea bream on a plank of wood. Josui scolded the man, saying, "If a man of your small stipend does something like this, your warrior's equipment will be incomplete, it will be difficult to care for your family and in the end you will have forgotten what obligation means." The man was flustered and replied, "No, no, this is something I received, and though it's a breach of etiquette, I thought of my lord, and so brought it here." Josui then said, "If that's so, please take this plank of fish and sell it. It's unnecessary to leave it here."

Again, when a melon was presented to him, he gave it to his pages to eat and had the rind pickled.

The furniture and utensils he used were likewise rather plain. Moreover, he would put a price on worn-out items and sell them off to his retainers. When a man who was close to him asked, "Rather than sell them off, why don't you just compel your inferiors to take them?" Josui just laughed. "Which is more pleasant—to receive something or to buy it yourself?" "To receive something is fine," the man replied, "but not as good as buying it yourself." Josui said, "That's likely so. Moreover, the man who receives something is going to be pleased, but the man who receives nothing is going to hold a grudge. It's just smarter to sell things off than it is to decide who gets something and who doesn't."

When you think too much, it will be difficult to win in a great battle. If you are too clever and look too far ahead, you will accomplish nothing in battle.

Close to death, Josui called Nagamasa to him. Saying, "A memento," he gave him something wrapped up in a purple silk cloth. When Nagamasa opened it, he found one straw sandal and one wooden clog. Josui intended to show that when you have either a pair of straw sandals or a pair of wooden clogs, you cannot throw them away. But if you have only one of each, you can discard both of them. Something that seems complete, then, is not complete at all. Every time you look at this pair, a single straw sandal and a single wooden clog, set your mind on resolution.

Kuroda Nagamasa
(1568–1623)

AT AGE SIXTEEN, Nagamasa fought for the forces of Hideyoshi at the Battle of Shizugatake, and at the age of twenty-two took over the administration of his province upon his father's retirement. He also took part in the Kyushu and Korean campaigns, and aided the Eastern Army at the Battle of Sekigahara.[1] Due to his meritorious deeds, he was awarded by Ieyasu with a large fief at Chikuzen in northern Kyushu. When imperial rule was restored to Japan with the Meiji Revolution of 1868, and the shogunate abolished, his descendants were granted the title of Marquis.

🔻   🔻   🔻

For someone's first time in seeing action in the field, there should be an understanding as to how to choose an opponent. When a man is not used to battle, it will be difficult for him if he meets with a strong enemy, and he may become timid and lose his sense of courage. For this reason, such a man should be directed to an opponent who is easily defeated. If his courage is thus nourished, he will later become brave and strong.

🔻   🔻   🔻

You must be careful about the appraisal of long and short swords, and in the very same way, you must also be careful

---

1. See note, page 78.

about your appraisal of men. Doing so, you will rarely make mistakes.

🌣   🌣   🌣

For the young men who will accompany you to battle for the first time, there are three levels on which you may try to appraise them. First, there may be ten men who appear to be manly, quite ready of wit and sure to do deeds that excel over others. Another ten may look weak, without talent and likely to be of no use. Yet another ten will seem to be neither especially courageous nor cowardly, and probably just the common run of men.

Well then, when these thirty men are put to the test of battle, the ten men of middling rank will prove to be as you appraised them: the common run of men who neither flee nor are victorious. Among the ten men you supposed to be of excellent abilities, eight or nine will be just as you thought and do great deeds, but one or two of them will turn out to be astonishing cowards. Moreover, of the ten men you judged to be of no particular use, eight or nine will be just as you thought, but one or perhaps two will be matchless brave men and go beyond even those you predicted would be excellent.

These one or two men were either mistakenly appraised or have a depth that our eyes cannot fathom.

🌣   🌣   🌣

When establishing lodging on a journey, first find a place on a wide part of the road; second, make it a place where you can complete whatever business you may have; and third, be conscious of the possibility of fire.

🌣   🌣   🌣

In a place where you should bring a spear, bring a spear; in a place where you should use a sword, use a sword; in a place where you should carry a short sword, carry a short sword. Each has its place.

Nagamasa was once departing from the front of his residence when his eyes were arrested by a sword rack with swords of more than three feet in length. When he asked whose swords they were, and was told that they belonged to foot soldiers, he was full of praise. "These are swords that give you a good feeling, "he said. "How fitting for young men."

When a young samurai, the son of a man with the stipend of three thousand *koku*, who was there by chance heard this remark, he thought that Nagamasa must have a liking for long swords and equipped himself with a sword over three feet in length.

One day, when Nagamasa was out hawking, the man was wearing this weapon of which he was quite proud, and walking around where the lord could see him. That night, Nagamasa had a meal made of the day's catch, invited his close vassals to join him and the conversation turned to the young samurai's sword that he had seen that day.

"It is important for people to be appropriate to the work that they have," he noted. "For a foot soldier to carry a long sword is according to his duty, but is it appropriate for the son of a man with a stipend of three thousand koku? This is not saying that he has to carry a spear" And he said the above words.

🔆 🔆 🔆

Whether a man be of high or low status, it is especially important that he be mindful of thrift. Because a man of low status has a small stipend, if he does not act with thrift he will soon find himself in extremities. In this way, it is easy

for him to be thrifty on his own. A man of high status, however, may spend lavishly, but not get into difficulties. Being
thrifty will be difficult for him and he will be unaware of the
poverty in his heart.

🔹   🔹   🔹

True thrift is hating the smallest waste, but having no regret
in spending even a large sum on something useful.

Once, returning to his home province from Edo, Nagamasa
stopped in Fushimi and was given the gift of a sea bass. He called
the cook and ordered him to prepare a little for the evening meal,
and then pickle the remainder in salt to eat on the boat home.

That evening, a local official visited Nagamasa to return
some money. Formerly, the man had been in difficult straits and
borrowed a fairly large sum from Nagamasa, The latter, however,
refused to accept it, and had the man return home and take the
money with him.

Comparing these two incidents, a close retainer looked du-
biously at Nagamasa, who said the above words.

🔹   🔹   🔹

It is best to understand the sword as something by which you
will die. If you think of it as something that will save your
life, you will either be defeated or you will not be reflecting
on your everyday situation.

🔹   🔹   🔹

Once a month, Nagamasa would gather the clan elders and five
or six other men, and initiate an informal evening chat. He called

these occasions "Admonition Meetings," or "Meetings Without Anger." At these gatherings, Nagamasa would first say, "Tonight, no matter what is said, there should be no remaining malice, and no revealing it to others. And of course, no one should get angry. You should not hold back anything that comes to mind."

After Nagamasa promised this himself, and all the others did the same, the meeting always progressed. It is said that the subject matter of these talks began with criticisms of Nagamasa, and then went on to things that would ordinarily have been difficult to express.

Todo Takatora
(1556–1630)

TAKATORA, an ardent Buddhist, was the descendant of a daimyo family distantly related to the imperial family. He first served Oda Nobunaga, and after the latter's death, Toyotomi Hideyoshi. At the age of thirty-five, he entered the priesthood at the temple settlement on Mount Koya, but was recalled by Hideyoshi to become counselor to an heir of the Oda clan. During Hideyoshi's invasion of Korea, Takatora was put in command of part of the Japanese fleet. In 1594, he returned to Mount Koya, but was recalled yet again by Hideyoshi, and became warlord of a series of fiefs. At the Battle of Sekigahara,[1] he switched his allegiance to the Eastern Army of Tokugawa Ieyasu, and was duly rewarded with a large fief at Tsu. His descendants remained there until the Meiji Revolution of 1868, when the shogunate was abolished and they were granted the title of Count.

There are some men who treat their wives coldly. If there is a reason that they should separate from them, then they should do so. If there is no such reason, they should treat them with affection.

A man who treats his wife coldly will perhaps be a cold person himself, and is not to be relied upon.

---

1. See note, page 78.

Takatora expressed this opinion to his close retainers, one that ran counter to the feudalistic Confucian worldview and flew in the face of reputation.

🔺　　🔺　　🔺

When you arise from your bed in the morning, you should understand that the day of your death has arrived. If you will be resolved in this manner, when you do sleep, you will be shaken by nothing.

🔺　　🔺　　🔺

You should understand that small things are great, and great things are small.

Takatora believed that when you think that something is unimportant, you may be negligent, and the matter will become more imposing than it should have been. With matters of great importance, you should not become so cautious that you fail.

🔺　　🔺　　🔺

As a superior, if you have doubts about your subordinates, they, in turn, will have doubts about you. When there are mutual doubts between superior and subordinates, their hearts will become mutually estranged. Though the ruler may be the main pillar, if those beneath him are estranged, he cannot stand alone; and during important times, there will be no samurai to serve him. Moreover, if evil men perceive this estrangement between high and low, they will find it an opportunity for slander.

Tokugawa Ieyasu had a high regard for Takatora, and encouraged his own son Hidetada to listen to the things that Takatora said. Hidetada would invite Takatora to his residence for nightly conversations and at such times, Takatora would lecture on "the Way of the Ruler."

Five years after the fall of Osaka Castle, Hidetada wanted to repair the Nijo palace, which served as a residence for the shoguns when they visited Kyoto. He ordered Takatora to draw up designs for the reconstruction. Takatora presented two sets of plans, and then spoke to his close retainers, who wondered why he created two, rather than one.

I created and then presented two plans to the shogun so that he might consider and reference both. No matter which one he chooses, it will be one with which he is personally familiar. Had I only submitted one, it would be something that I myself had determined. This would not be respecting my superior. A person who is employed by another should make sure that his superior receives the credit for something that turns out well, but he himself should take the blame for something that turns out poorly. To make a display of your own merits and neglect the virtues of your superior is to invite envy and backbiting. You should be circumspect in such things.

The two warlords Takatora and Kuroda Nagamasa did not get along well. But when someone once called on Takatora and criticized Nagamasa, Takatora turned red and said angrily,

My relationship with him is not at all good, but I have never once spoken ill of him behind his back. Do you think you would make me happy by criticizing him?

🔺　　　🔺　　　🔺

Here is another story demonstrating Takatora's relationships with others. Directly after the Battle of Sekigahara, Ishida Mitsunari had been captured and was about to be executed when someone from the Eastern Army began to insult him. In quite a different fashion, Takatora approached Mitsunari courteously and exchanged reminiscences with him about the old days. Takatora then said,

My own preparations for battle are not understood from the point of view of my allies. For my own reference and for the sake of our old friendship, tell me how they are seen by you, my enemy.

Mitsunari readily replied,

"The leader of your advanced guard of gunners appeared to be a man of low rank. Now the actions of a man will differ according to his high or low status. What do you think it will be like when the enemy is clearly aware of this?"

It is said that Takatora quickly raised the leader of the gunners' stipend by a good sum.

Hachisuka Iemasa
(1598–1638)

HACHISUKA IEMASA, a Christian, was the descendant of an ancient and powerful clan in the central Japan province of Owari. Together with his father, he served Toyotomi Hideyoshi, achieved many meritorious deeds, and after the pacification of the island of Shikoku, he and his father became lords of the castle at Tokushima. Later, he took part in Hideyoshi's invasion of Korea. At the Battle of Sekigahara,[1] Iemasa was allied with the Western Army of the Toyotomi clan, but refrained from engaging in the battle, sending his son, Yoshishige to join the Eastern Army of the Tokugawa clan. Therefore, after the battle, he continued to hold his old fief without incident. His descendants became lords of the castle at Awa, and remained in Tokushima until the Meiji Revolution of 1868, when the shogunate was abolished and they received the title of Marquis.

If there is something that should be done slowly, there will be no great harm in doing it quickly. But if there is something that should be done quickly, there will be great harm in doing it slowly.

1. See note, page 78.

Today, I should be returning to my residence in the evening. In the meantime, if you have some place you would like to go, please do so. You should come back by nightfall.

Once, when Iemasa had returned to Edo, he was invited to the mansion of another daimyo. On setting out, he gave his retainers some spending money and spoke to them in this way, showing a certain amount of human-heartedness on Iemasa's part.

🔹   🔹   🔹

There was a certain retainer who, due to illness, had not attended upon Iemasa for a long time. By chance one day, he felt a bit better, took a walk nearby and suddenly encountered Iemasa's retinue. Iemasa said, "I've heard that you've been sick for a long time. What kind of illness have you had?" The retainer became flurried, fearing that Iemasa was thinking that his illness had been feigned, and answered "I've been suffering from deafness."

Deafness, of course, means the loss of the sense of hearing, but to instantaneously come up with an illness that was no impediment to walking around outside was a slip of the tongue. Iemasa, however, left right away with a simple, "Take care of yourself." After that, the retainer sorely regretted what he had said, but there was nothing to be done. Now he could only worry and be at a loss.

Nevertheless, the next day, Iemasa sent a messenger to inquire after the man's health with the present of a fish. "Your face looked a bit haggard," the messenger quoted, "and you seemed rather thin and pale. You must be feeling gloomy, so please get better."

The retainer felt relieved and soon recovered altogether. For his part, Iemasa had felt that, regretting his slip of the tongue, the retainer would become increasingly ill, and so sent the messenger to visit him.

Although Iemasa was known for this sort of psychological insight and warmheartedness, he also tested his vassals and retainers in different ways. Once, for example, when the winter was quite cold, Iemasa called over a close retainer and said, "Your feet must be cold. I was thinking of giving you some *tabi*[2] that I've worn for a long time, but I could only find one of the pair. For the time being, go ahead and take this one."

Days went by, and about the time the incident would have passed out of his mind, the retainer was called once again. This time, Iemasa said, "I found the other tabi and would like to give it to you. Please bring me the one that I gave to you the other day."

The man had not lost or misplaced it, and brought it to Iemasa, who thereupon increased the man's stipend.

---

2. *Tabi*: Japanese-style socks in which the big toe is separated from the others.

Terasawa Hirotaka
(1564–1633)

HIROTAKA FIRST SERVED under Toyotomi Hideyoshi, and fought under the latter's forces in the campaign to pacify Kyushu.[1] For his efforts he was awarded with the castle at Karatsu in Hizen Province. He also took part in Hideyoshi's invasion of Korea and achieved many meritorious deeds. In the Battle of Sekigahara,[2] he fought in the side of the Eastern Army and for this was awarded with control of the Amakusa Islands. After Sekigahara, Hirotaka continued construction on Karatsu Castle and laid the base for the flourishing town Karatsu is today. Tragically, his son and successor, Katataka, harshly oppressed the people of the area and brought upon the Shimabara Rebellion. The rebellion was successfully suppressed, but at some cost, and Katataka was dispossessed. He soon committed suicide, bringing about the end of Hirotaka's line.

☗   ☗   ☗

Now when a man ascends a castle or climbs a mountain and looks down on people, others do not blame or resent him. When a man builds a second or third story to his mansion, climbs to the top and looks down on people, he is both blamed and resented. Moreover, when a man is proud of his

---

1. The Kyushu campaign: when Hideyoshi sent a large army into Kyushu in 1587 to weaken the power of the local lords, particularly the powerful Shimazu clan. It was from a pacified Kyushu that he would later launch his attack on Korea.
2. See note, page 78.

wit and intelligence, he is detested and resented as well. A man of high estate is not resented or blamed if his status is natural and not a created one.

      🔺   🔺   🔺

If a man wants to achieve some merit, he must abandon his own predilections. If he holds on to his own likes and dislikes, his work will be done negligently.

      🔺   🔺   🔺

If you only hear about something and do not see it for yourself, you will not come to the last word on its profit or loss, its advantage or disadvantage,

Hosokawa Tadaoki
(1563–1645)

TADAOKI WAS KNOWN AS a general, strategist, tea master and poet. He was the son of Hosokawa Yusai. His wife Gracia was the daughter of Akechi Mitsuhide, whose betrayal and attack on his lord, Oda Nobunaga in the Honnoji Temple Incident brought about the latter's suicide. Mitsuhide was in turn killed shortly thereafter by the forces of Hideyoshi. Tadaoki waited out these difficulties as the lord of Miyazu Castle in Tango. After Hideyoshi's death, he allied himself with Tokugawa Ieyasu and became lord of the Ogura Castle in Buzen. His son, Tadatoshi, was granted the fief at the castle at Kumamoto with a stipend of 540,000 *koku* and his descendants continued there until the Meiji Restoration in 1868.

Retainers should be thought of as the players in shogi. The players have various moves [. . .] and men, too, are like this. Though one man may not be good at one particular function, he can be employed at something else. This is the same as the Duke of Chou[1] telling his son, Pai Ch'in, "Do not seek for one man to possess all talents." Not one man in a hundred

---

1. The Duke of Chou was the brother of the first ruler of the Chou dynasty, King Wu of Chou (1122–770 BC). When the king died, leaving only a very young son as heir, the Duke of Chou became regent, and is considered to have been a paragon of virtue and one of the most influential persons of his time.

can be successful in all situations, and a lord and everyone else should understand this."

This was the technique of leadership Tadaoki taught to his son Tadatoshi.

🔺   🔺   🔺

You can instruct a retainer twice, but on the third time, dismiss him.[2]

Tadaoki was asked by his good friend, Nagai Hyuga-no-kami, "Your retainers are all orderly and sharp. What kind of training do you use on them?" Tadaoki answered, "I instruct them two times. If this is ineffective, I dismiss them. Maybe that's why their behavior is so good."

🔺   🔺   🔺

I would call a man good who is like an oyster shell in Akashi Bay.

This was Tadaoki's response when the second Tokugawa shogun, Hidetada, asked Tadaoki, "What kind of man would you consider an splendid one?"

Hidetada nodded his assent, but his councilors who were seated there did not understand at all.

On a later day, Hidetada explained it to them. "It seems that you did not understand what Tadaoki said. This is to say that the oyster shells in the bay are buffeted back and forth by the waves

---

2. The original Japanese word 切り申し候 (*kirimoshi*) can mean "to cut him down" or "to cut connections with." The latter translation seems more in line with Tadaoki's character.

and their edges are rounded off. A man is also buffeted by others and thus comes to have an excellent character."

∧   ∧   ∧

The administration of a ruler should be like putting a round lid on a square container.

When Tadaoki was asked by Hidetada what his understanding of a good administration would be, this was his reply, meaning that if a government allows no margin, people will feel suffocated.

Date Masamune
(1567–1636)

WHEN YOUNG, Masamune suffered from smallpox and lost the use of one eye, for which he earned the name "the One-eyed Dragon." Born the son of the lord of Yonezawa Castle, he expanded his clan's influence in the northern region of Japan and established a residence at what would become Aizu Wakamatsu Castle. He was distrusted by Toyotomi Hideyoshi, and forced to move back to Yonezawa. Although he took part in the invasion of Korea, he was accused of disloyalty to Hideyoshi, but managed to free himself from any charges. At the Battle of Sekigahara,[1] he fought for the Eastern Army and was awarded with a large fief and a castle which he named Sendai. At first friendly toward Christians, he changed his stance to avoid the displeasure of the shogun. He is said to have been a protector of artists and scholars.

　　　🔱　　　🔱　　　🔱

When all is going well with a warrior, it is best that he make sure that there are no wants or inconveniences within his fief and his family mansion. But if something unsavory should occur, he should return to his province and family domicile, clean the dust from all places that cannot ordinarily be seen, complete repairs to the house, make sure of all the affairs and laws of the province, clearly direct that all damaged places should be repaired, then depart.

---

1. See note, page 78.

🔺　　　🔺　　　🔺

Throughout my life, I was never taken aback by anything. But when I heard that this tea bowl was so extraordinarily high-priced, I was totally fascinated, taken aback and then mortified.

Masamune once was inspecting a tea bowl, nearly dropped it and was given a shock. It is said that right after this occurred, he took the tea bowl out and smashed it against a stone in the garden.

🔺　　　🔺　　　🔺

With momentous events, it is better not to discuss the matter with others, but to be thoroughly secure in your own decision.

Masamune once spoke reminiscently to close vassals about three momentous occasions in his life when he achieved excellent results by making a decision on his own:

"When the Taiko [Hideyoshi][2] was attacking Odawara Castle in 1590, I hurried to Odawara thinking he might trust me to join him. My retainers asked if I shouldn't be worried and counseled me to establish a strategic position to defend and protect myself from his possible attack. I told them, no, the Taiko is not an ordinary man and I would show him an attitude of submission. Thus, I departed for the front. My retainers then advised I should be accompanied by a large force, but I went to Odawara with only ten mounted men. These I left at a proper distance and had an audience with the Taiko. Then, without incident, I returned to my own province. In this way, I was aided by my own resolution.

---

2. Taiko: a respectful form of address for a regent, mainly used for Hideyoshi. Hideyoshi was never allowed to take the title of shogun because he had no ancestral connections with the Genji (Minamoto) clan.

"The next time was when the Kanpaku [chief advisor to the emperor], Lord Hidetsugu[3] was ordered to commit suicide. I was held in doubt by the Taiko and went to the capital to explain myself. Three envoys came to my lodging to investigate me, but I declared, 'The Taiko's discernment is different from my own, and the Kanpaku has been relieved of his office; and it is natural that, having only one eye, I have mistakenly been friendly with the man. If you think that is wrong, there is nothing else to be done, so please cut off my head.' The envoys asked me to please not say such a thing, but I spoke roughly with them and ordered them to relate my words just as they were to the Taiko. The next day I was ordered to the castle, but was served tea by the Taiko, who was in a very good humor.

"The third time was some years later when I served tea to Lord Iemitsu. Tea master and well-known samurai Sakuma Shokan brought the tea canister into the kitchen and said, 'Use this for the tea. It's something given to you by the shogun himself.' He suggested this two or three times, but I steadfastly refused, and when I went out to greet Iemitsu, he presented me with the tea canister with his own hands. I received it humbly and said, 'A little while ago, I heard from Shokan that I was honored with a gift from you, but I felt it an act of irreverence to receive it in the kitchen, and so did not accept it.' Iemitsu seemed quite impressed with this.

"On these three occasions, I persevered with my own thoughts rather than listen to the advice of others."

---

3. Hidetsugu: the nephew of Hideyoshi, whom the latter designated as his successor until his own son was born. Hidetsugu was eventually accused by Hideyoshi of plotting against him and was ordered to commit suicide. There was a rumor that Masamune, who was friendly with Hidetsugu, was a co-conspirator in this plot and would be ordered to commit suicide as well.

Sanada Nobuyuki
(1566–1658)

NOBUYUKI WAS THE eldest son of Sanada Masayuki, the lord of Ueda Castle. At the Battle of Sekigahara,[1] he fought on the side of the Eastern Army, while his father and younger brother Yukimura joined the Western Army. After the Eastern Army had won, both Masayuki and Yukimura were condemned to death, but through the intervention of Nobuyuki, they were pardoned and exiled to Mount Koya. Nobuyuki, however, was given an extra allowance and appointed as the lord of Ueda Castle. It is said that the strategy of dividing the family's allegiances between the Eastern and Western armies was a desperate measure to insure the continuance of the family regardless of which side won. Before Sekigahara, Ieyasu had given Nobuyuki in marriage to the daughter of his retainer Honda Tadakatsu, and as a result Nobuyuki had been inclined to take up Ieyasu's side. Nobuyuki was later transferred to Matsushiro in Shinano Province. When imperial rule was restored to Japan with the Meiji Revolution of 1868, and the shogunate abolished, his descendants were granted the title of Count.

When giving a man a high stipend because of his abilities, there is something you should think about. For that talented man's single generation, it is a fine thing, but that talent will have no connection with his descendants. This is to say

---

1. See note, page 78.

that to have an inherited high stipend diminish would be unfortunate. Thus, when you plan on granting high stipends, select samurai from your retainers, and there should be a number of excellent men. And you will have the advantage of the gratitude, not only of the men themselves, but of their entire families.

🔱　　🔱　　🔱

Sanada Nobuyuki was a very different kind of general. He would inform a vassal that he was coming to his mansion for a visit, and when the day was soon at hand, he would ask, "What kind of preparations are you making?" Then, he would have the estimation of the preparation expenses written out and include a note, "I planned to visit you, but it's inconvenient right now. So please just give me a cash payment,"

Rather than having their lord come to their houses, the vassals were always happy to end things lightly with a payment of money, a discreet obligation. Over time, this became an annual event, and the amount was gradually increased.

One day, Nobuyuki was speaking to a close retainer and asked, "Surely there must be talk about me being stingy, mustn't there?" The retainer could hardly say that there was indeed, but instead replied, "It is said that you're wealthy." Whereupon, Nobuyuki said,

When spurring your soldiers on, you will not be able to do so by commands alone. If you do not gladly spend your resources and only yell out commands, your battles will come to naught. A warrior should be careful with his money.

Sanada Yukimura
(1567–1615)

YUKIMURA WAS A courageous general who stuck strongly to
his principles, even in the face of certain death, and has been a
popular subject of professional storytellers and folklore. He was
not simply a brave and heroic man. Though born the child of
a daimyo, he had experienced being a ronin, and saw through
the vicissitudes of changing fortunes. He fought for the Western
Army during the Battle of Sekigahara,[1] and blocked Tokugawa
Hidetada, third son of Ieyasu, as his forces attempted to descend
the Nakasendo mountain road. After the battle, Yukimura was
exiled to Mount Koya for over ten years. When Ieyasu decided
to destroy the remnants of the Toyotomi clan at Osaka Castle, he
recalled Yukimura, who instead joined the defenders of the castle
and died with its destruction.

＊　　　＊　　　＊

Once a promise is made, you can compare its weight in this
way: you would not change your allegiance even for half of
Japan, much less for the province of Shinano.

Fourteen years after the Battle of Sekigahara, Ieyasu, who
had been waiting for the right moment, finally marched toward
Osaka Castle to destroy the Toyotomi. Certainly he viewed
Yukimura, who had taken command of the castle after his exile
at Mount Koya, as a menace.

---

1. See note, page 78.

Of the generals who had received the kindness of Hide-yoshi, whose clan had now been destroyed, some had died, some were old, and though the control of the country had fallen to the Tokugawa, Ieyasu could still not afford to be negligent. Though the vast majority of warlords were considered to be loyal to the Tokugawa, there were still powerful daimyo like the Shimazu, Maeda and Kato—some fourteen in all—who had been close to the Toyotomi. Of course none of these would directly oppose the Tokugawa shogunate, but how they would react during the course of a battle was unknown.

Thus, Ieyasu sent Yukimura's uncle, Sanada Nobutada, to parley with Yukimura. With their first meeting, Yukimura was promised a stipend of 30,000 *koku* if he would change his mind and come over to the Tokugawa side. During the second meeting he was promised the entire province of Shinano.

Yukimura's response, quoted above, was sent back to the shogun.

🔱　　🔱　　🔱

No negligence whatsoever should be permitted in regards to retainers. There may be many lies and deceits among parents and children, and brothers and sisters, as they are led astray by desire for profit. Nevertheless, though retainers are not connected by blood, they will have a sense of obligation, respect the power of their lord and follow orders and give their lives for him. Thus, one must be extremely mindful when choosing retainers.

In the most casual conversation, if a lord should carelessly mention a personal pleasure, a retainer may try to take advantage of the resonance of that pleasure and plan his own worldly success. Seeing through to the lord's hidden feelings and handling him like a puppet would be regrettable.

Kimura Shigenari
(1593–1615)

SHIGENARI WAS BORN to a daimyo in Yamashiro Province who was eventually dispossessed and committed suicide. From a young age he was employed by Hideyoshi's son Toyotomi Hideyori, and at the time of the peace treaty ending the winter campaign against Osaka Castle, acted as a messenger between the two hostile parties. In the succeeding summer campaign, he met a heroic death. A handsome young man, his demise was regretted even by the Tokugawa, and he was spoken of with admiration by the common folk as well.

During the peace negotiations after the winter campaign, the state of affairs was tense and the Tokugawa began to consider a next assault. In April 1615, Ieyasu gathered a huge army and surrounded the castle, whose defenders numbered less than half of the Tokugawa forces. Moreover, although one of the conditions of the peace negotiations was that the outer moat would be filled in, Ieyasu began to destroy the stone walls of the outworks, which would leave almost no structural impediments to the siege and destruction of the castle.

As the final battle neared, Shigenari began to have less of an appetite. When his wife questioned him about it, he replied,

My enemies will very likely take my head. I intend not to leave an unsightly corpse, and so am being careful about my meals.

Shigenari was struck down with the fall of the castle, but it is said that his hair was imbued with an elegant fragrance.

Tachibana Muneshige
(1569–1642)

MUNESHIGE WAS AN influential warlord in Kyushu and the lord of Yanagawa Castle in the province of Chikugo. He took part in Hideyoshi's invasion of Korea where he defeated a Chinese battalion and came to the rescue of Kato Kiyomasa whose troops had been defeated at Ulsan. At the Battle of Sekigahara,[1] he fought for the Western Army and, after their defeat, was dispossessed. Later, he was pardoned and given a small fief in the northern part of Japan. At the siege of Osaka Castle, he joined the forces of Tokugawa Ieyasu, performed meritorious deeds and, as a reward, was reinstated in his old fief in Kyushu. Both Munashige and his son Tadanari fought those who rebelled against the cruelty of the local lord in the insurrection at Shimabara. When imperial rule was restored to Japan with the Meiji Revolution of 1868, and the shogunate abolished, his descendants were granted the title of Count.

If you will do first what your opponent is about to do, you will not be without victory.

Tachibana Muneshige was an accomplished strategist, and often put the above words into practice during actual battle. He became famous for this in particular for his part in the suppression of the insurrection at Kumamoto.

---

1. See note, page 78.

Hideyoshi's pacification of Kyushu ended with the submission of the Shimazu clan, but the state of affairs throughout the island was not completely settled. The strength of the Kumamoto insurrection was surprising: two of Muneshige's branch castles were surrounded and the supply roads cut off. The reinforcements were attacked and the generals taken as prisoners.

At this point, Muneshige, then at the neighboring Yanagawa Castle, was ordered by Hideyoshi to take action. Muneshige took the initiative by hiding a corps of gunners in a strategic place where the insurrectionists were likely to attack, and, with an air of ignorance, started off for the branch castles with supplies. The gunnery corps lay in wait for the insurrectionists as the latter approached the location where they were sure to attack. With a single massive volley, the tables were turned and the supplies were delivered without incident. With this as a start, Muneshige suppressed the insurrection altogether.

◆   ◆   ◆

If your residence is too imposing, your subordinates will hesitate to approach you. In the same way, if your possessions are too gaudy, both the upper and lower classes will have a strong sense of estrangement, and the superiors will not be known to the inferiors, nor the inferiors to the superiors.

At the Battle of Sekigahara, Muneshige sided with the Western Army, incurred the wrath of Ieyasu and was dispossessed of his fief at Yanagawa. Fourteen years later, at the siege of Osaka Castle, however, he was pardoned due to his meritorious deeds and in 1620 returned to his old fief. In the twenty years since he had resided at Yanagawa Castle the fief had been granted to military commander Tanaka Yoshimasa as a reward for his capture of Ishida Mitsunari, but Yoshimasa later incurred the hostility of

Ieyasu because of his mismanagement of the fief. On his return to the castle, however, Muneshige saw that Yoshimasa had completely reconstructed everything, from the castle itself down to the residences of the samurai, now luxurious beyond recognition.

When he heard that Muneshige had been reinstated in his former fief, the neighboring daimyo, Nabeshima Katsushige, came to congratulate him. After Katsushige had returned home, one of Muneshige's retainers commented, "Lord Tanaka did you a favor by rebuilding the castle and samurai residences so beautifully. Our guests will be impressed."

Muneshige responded with the above quote, and then added, "It was exactly this unnecessary thing that caused his ruin."

🔺　　🔺　　🔺

It's not good to brag about something small. What will a person of understanding think when he hears you?

During a certain battle, a samurai from another fief distinguished himself by taking the head of an enemy. However, it was Muneshige's forces that had set up the opportunity for this, and one of his retainers spoke of his chagrin about this fact. Muneshige reproved him, saying, "To claim credit for something after the fact is unbecoming," and continued with the above words.

🔺　　🔺　　🔺

No matter what it is, whether you think it's good or bad, speak in the same manner, whether it's to your wife, your retainers or even to messengers to other lords. From the very beginning, there should not be even a hair's breadth of something hidden. In the bedroom and even with secondary retainers, speak your mind.

Matsukura Shigemasa
(1574–1630)

SHIGEMASA WAS FIRST ATTACHED to the daimyo Tsutsui Sadaie in Yamato Province, then served Tokugawa Ieyasu. Achieving meritorious deeds at the Battle of Sekigahara[1] and the siege of Osaka Castle, he was awarded the castle and fief of Shimabara in Kyushu. When some of his ships were blown off course and landed at Luzon, he at first set up communications with the inhabitants of the islands, but later requested permission from the Tokugawa government to launch an expedition against the Philippines. This was granted, but Shigemasa died before it was put into effect.

Shigemasa was a brave and ferocious general, but persecuted the Christians in Shimabara, and seven years after his death, an insurrection occurred which combined the strength of the suppressed peasants and the Christian community, and in the end had to be put down by an expensive force of troops from throughout Japan. When peace finally returned with the destruction of the insurrectionists, Shigemasa's son, Shigeharu, was dispossessed of his castle and fief and eventually committed suicide.

🔺   🔺   🔺

When you employ someone, if you do not give him some sort of job, his mind will grow slack, and his time will be spent sleeping. Order him to some duty, no matter what it might be.

---

1. See note, page 78.

Shigemasa ordered each of his retainers to some position, even if it was just being in charge of the ashtrays and taking good care of his pipes. He felt that if a man did not have a determined role, he would become uneasy.[2]

A   A   A

We lesser daimyo gather and even eat together with all of our retainers. This is because if something unexpected happens, we could depart for the front right away. In the end, with warriors, there is no difference between high and low estate.

Shigemasa welcomed ronin, would call them together and eat unpolished rice with them. His success at the siege of Osaka Castle is said to have been due to such men.

A   A   A

Here is a story about the relationships among Shigemasa's retainers. In his household there were two retainers who got along extraordinarily well. One of them had a stipend of 300 *koku*, the other, a stipend of 400.[3] One day, the man with 300 koku protested his stipend and absconded. Shigemasa called in the man with 400 koku, and, giving him travel expenses, ordered him to pursue the absconder. "No matter how many years it takes," he said, "track down the man and arrest him."

The man took his leave of Shigemasa, but was shedding tears. When the latter inquired about this, the man said, "When my friend hears that I have been ordered to pursue him, he will likely

---

2. This is not dissimilar to the quote "If the common man is idle, he will do something untoward," from the Confucian text *The Great Learning*, attributed to Zengzi, a disciple of Confucius.

3. One *koku* is equivalent to about five bushels of rice.

return right away and commit seppuku. I can't help weeping because that's so sad."

In the end, after a few days, the man who had absconded reappeared and was forgiven by Shigemasa, who then increased both of their stipends to five hundred koku.

Tokugawa Hidetada
(1579–1632)

HIDETADA WAS THE third son of Ieyasu and the second Tokugawa shogun. Although a comparatively quiet and modest man, he
succeeded his father at the young age of twenty-seven, and was
able to keep the generals and daimyo of the other provinces in
line, laying the foundation of the Tokugawa hegemony. Hidetada
persecuted the Christians, and shut Japan off to communication
with all foreigners except the Chinese, Dutch and Koreans.

If you have employed a man, do not dismiss him for some
fault he has committed. Forgive him and he will amend his
ways on his own.

Hidetada also said, "Today he may be bad, but tomorrow he'll
turn out well. You should wait, and treat him like a good man."

In recent times, Nobunaga exceeded everyone in his courage
and daring. Nevertheless, he only liked people to follow him
and hated to submit to others. Thus his unthinkable disaster.

This was not just saying that the common judgment of Nobunaga was correct, but was rather a comment on what the mind
of a commander should be. Hidetada further commented on his
father Ieyasu.

He could be tough or flexible in his assessment of affairs, and was able to perceive the various abilities of others and put them to use accordingly. Thus he was able to accomplish the great work of the country.

🔱　　🔱　　🔱

There is a saying that goes, "This floating world is like a dream. One step ahead is only darkness, so man should enjoy each moment." This is misleading. It is exactly because life is so short that each moment should be respected. And again, just because it is so short, it should be easy to be discreet.

🔱　　🔱　　🔱

In war and everything else, if you face it thinking, "This is interesting," you will lose all fear, and your strategies will come on their own.

Maeda Toshitsune
(1593–1658)

TOSHITSUNE WAS THE third generation of daimyo at Kaga, one of the wealthiest fiefs under the Tokugawa shogunate, inheriting it from his older brother, Toshinaga. Although too young to have engaged in any of the battles of the Warring States period, he participated in the siege of Osaka at the age of twenty. He retired to Komatsu Castle at the age of forty-six, but continued to encourage the industrial development of his fief. When imperial rule was restored to Japan with the Meiji Revolution of 1868, and the shogunate abolished, his descendants were granted the title of Marquis.

⚜   ⚜   ⚜

If a man lets a show of intelligence be manifest at the tip of his nose, he will cause anxiety to others, sow doubt about his high rank, and bring on unexpected disasters. In showing people that I am a bit of a fool, I can administer three provinces in a friendly way and put the common folk at ease.

Toshitsune always let his nose hairs grow out quite long. His retainers thought that this was a bit out of place with his status, and could not remain indifferent to his looks. They would pull out their own nose hairs when they were alone at night, hoping somehow that Toshitsune would get the hint. The lord, however, pretended not to notice.

At last, at Toshitsune's bath one night, a close retainer offered him a pair of tweezers. Seeing this, Toshitsune called all of his retainers together and said,

"A man who lets his nose hairs grow out is considered a fool by the world, and I know well that all of you think that my nose hairs are a bit strange. But please listen to my reason for leaving them as they are." He then went on to make the above quote. His retainers were taken aback by his words.

🔺   🔺   🔺

It is more appropriate for an eighteen-year-old to have the resources of an eighteen-year-old.

A close retainer once praised a young man, saying, "He's only eighteen, but there are few elders with his strength of character." Toshitsune rebuked the retainer with the above words.

🔺   🔺   🔺

A general should not speak thoughtlessly or at random to his retainers. With a sudden emergency, there should be nothing else to add. Any words that are spoken at this time should encourage the soldiers to make light of death.

Tokugawa Yorinobu
(1602–1671)

TOKUGAWA YORINOBU WAS THE tenth son of the first Tokugawa shogun, Ieyasu. He was extraordinarily talented, and was much loved by Ieyasu. Yorinobu became the first of the Tokugawa lords of Kii, a line from which three shoguns were chosen. He worked hard at increasing agricultural production in his domain, and was responsible for compiling and editing codes of law. He married a daughter of daimyo Kato Kiyomasa. When imperial rule was restored to Japan with the Meiji Revolution of 1868, and the shogunate abolished, his descendants were granted the title of Marquis.

🔱   🔱   🔱

Do you think I'll ever be fourteen again?

During the summer campaign against Osaka Castle in 1615, Tokugawa Ieyasu allowed the young Yorinobu to accompany the army, but placed him in the rear guard so that he would not be involved in any direct action. When the fighting was over, Yorinobu cried bitterly. Matsudaira Masatsuna, one of Ieyasu's vassals, tried to comfort the boy, and said, "Don't be in such a hurry. You're still young, so you'll have plenty of opportunities to fight later on." Yorinobu only glared at Masatsuna and replied, "What are you saying! Do you think I'll ever be fourteen again?"

When Ieyasu heard about this, he straightened up in his chair and said, "These words are like a spear!"

In using wise and brave men, listen to what they say. This will stand you in good stead, for the vast wisdom and discrimination of all your vassals will become your own.

This is said to have been one of Yorinobu's favorite sayings.

You should not think the man who is praised to be good, or the man who is spoken ill of to be bad. A good general should keep this in mind.

A vassal once praised a certain man to Yorinobu, and recommended him highly. Yorinobu, however, made no reply. The vassal once again repeated his recommendation of the man, but Yorinobu remained silent. When the vassal persisted a third time, Yorinobu responded with the above words.

- **Do not try to get in a man's good graces.**
- **Do not cling to your own opinions.**
- **Don't let your mind be absent.**

These precepts from Yorinobu have been called *The Three Articles that Enlightened the Vassal.*

A man becomes "one who has arrived" by understanding death. The man who has passed sixty years of age, and still plots and schemes, does not know himself. By not knowing himself, how will he understand others?

Yorinobu here refers to the *Analects of Confucius*, where the sage comments, "At fifteen, I had the will to study; at thirty, I knew where to stand; at forty, I was no longer confused; at fifty, I knew Heaven's decree; at sixty, I listened humbly to others; and at seventy, I followed what my heart desired, but did not transgress the Law."

Tokugawa Yorifusa
(1603–1661)

YORIFUSA WAS TOKUGAWA IEYASU'S eleventh son. At the age of seven, he was made the lord of Mito Castle. At thirteen, he gained experience at an actual site of war when he participated in the summer siege of Osaka Castle. Even when a child, he had a surprising strength of spirit and, at age six, when Ieyasu asked him what he wanted, he replied, "The whole country."

🔥   🔥   🔥

Make what is good and beautiful all your own, but do not attribute your mistakes to the fault of others.

🔥   🔥   🔥

In the common world, *junshi* is considered to be a matter of gratitude. If someone does not commit junshi for a lord, he is called disloyal; and if one does not commit junshi for a vassal, he is said to be lacking in gratitude. This attitude should be understood to be inhumane. When I die, please prohibit this custom.

The practice of *junshi*, committing suicide at the death of one's lord, was common from the Warring States period to the early Edo period. When Yorifusa became ill, however, he beckoned his children and gave them this last command. After his death, the central government outlawed junshi for the entire country.

Tokugawa Iemitsu
(1604–1651)

THE THIRD TOKUGAWA SHOGUN, Iemitsu established the policy of a "closed country," allowing people neither in nor out of Japan. Once, on a rainy day, his grandfather Ieyasu ordered Iemitsu and his younger brother, Tadanaga, to go out into the garden. Lifting up his sleeve, Tadanaga went on out, but Iemitsu calmly went down into the garden just as he was. Ieyasu then ordered them to sit down. Tadanaga sat down, raising his sleeve higher and higher; but Iemitsu simply sat there, pelted by the rain. Seeing that Iemitsu's attitude was that he did not care about trifles, Ieyasu knew that he had the genius to maintain the country.

🔺 🔺 🔺

The Way of Jesus is, of course, a heresy; but if it contains words that people are liable to believe, you should pay attention to those who follow its teachings.

Iemitsu was a major prosecutor of Christianity, but these words spoken to daimyo Inoue Masashige, show his belief that regardless of what you find repugnant, you should judge things objectively and maintain an attitude of analysis in all things.

🔺 🔺 🔺

Every time you samurai get together, you will talk about various things and inevitably will make good and bad judgments on your companions. That being the case, some resentment

will be created and you should not be incautious about this matter. If this cannot be helped, you should then discuss your own shortcomings. Listening to your own faults, you should make amends.

When someone is praised by many people, he will not necessarily be a an excellent samurai. In this world, when one is both praised and criticized, he is likely to be a good warrior.

Iemitsu believed that person's reputation is unreliable and that men praised by all are not limited to splendid people; such people are what you call "everybody's friend." Among those who are praised and those who are criticized are certainly people of character. He continued:

It would be good to witness a trial. No matter how fairly the person is tried, the man winning the judgment will be praised, while the losing side will be spoken of badly. So when everyone tends to praise someone, I remain doubtful.

Ikeda Mitsumasa
(1609–1682)

MITSUMASA WAS LORD OF THE Bizen Okayama clan. At the
beginning of the Edo period (1615–1868), he stood out for his
economic insights. Mitsumasa was born nine years after the Battle of Sekigahara[1] and died during the rule of the fifth shogun
Tsunayoshi. Consulting with Kumazawa Banzan, the disciple of
the Confucian scholar Nakae Toju, he reformed the administration of the fief. This had an effect on the industrial development
of the area which has lasted to the present day.

🔺   🔺   🔺

**Being proud of your own wisdom, you will think that no one
has good sense like your own, you will dislike the words of
others, and will not have true wisdom at all.**

Mitsumasa often lent his ear to the words of his vassals, and
accepted their opinions.

🔺   🔺   🔺

One cold night, Mitsumasa was eating tangerines when the
fief physician, Shiomi Genzo, objected and said, "Cold food at
night will not do." Mitsumasa stopped eating and went back
inside, mumbling, "Well, well, that was close." A lady attendant
asked him about what had just transpired. Mitsumasa said, "I

---

1. See note, page 78.

know that the danger is trifling, but I was cautioned by Shiomi Genzo. That is all. If I had rebuked him, would anyone give me their opinion later on? That was the danger."

🔺   🔺   🔺

If you do not have kindness, all your dignity will be of no use. If you do not have dignity, kindness will be of no use either. Dignity without compassion is useless. Compassion without dignity will be of no good.

Mitsumasa himself explained these words over and over in different ways.

When a lord only has kindness, but lacks dignity, his underlings, like children, will be pampered but will not listen. But again, if he only has dignity, they will follow him on the surface, but will not be attached to him in their hearts.

Again, Mitsumasa, with his emphasis on kindness and dignity, was not the average lord of a fief. This was also manifested in his other sayings.

One must display both kindness and dignity. But in the end, it is most important to know the lives of those beneath you. If you do not, neither kindness not dignity will be of any use.

Matsudaira Masayuki
(1611–1672)

PROGENITOR OF THE Aizu Matsudaira clan, Masayuki was the fourth child of the second Tokugawa shogun, Hidetada, was enfeoffed with a stipend of 230,000 *koku* and lived in Wakamatsu Castle. He established the foundation of the *Fifteen Clan Precepts*, which, if followed by his heirs and vassals, would preserve and strengthen the fief throughout the generations. Masayuki's descendants were active in supporting the peaceful transition of government at the end of the Tokugawa shogunate.

***

If someone tries to shame you, there will naturally be blame. With blame, comes the resolution to fight.

In 1652, laws were being adjusted in the Aizu Matsudaira clan. Clan officials presented drafts to the clan lord, Masayuki, but among them was an article prohibiting "fights and altercations." Masayuki looked at this and, thinking this would make for enervated men, struck it out and wrote the following:

Fights and altercations, for the most part, are punitive matters for both sides. It is unreasonable that both sides should be punished. A one-sided altercation should be punished.

Fights were, therefore, not prohibited, and if opponents mutually found fault, then fair fights were allowed. In later years, this was seen as the seed of the "Aizu warrior."

Tokugawa Mitsukuni
(1628–1700)

MITSUKUNI WAS THE INTELLIGENT, cultured and scholastic head of the Mito fief, north of Edo. He encouraged the study of history, literature and antiquities. It was Mitsukuni who began the monumental historical work, *Dai Nihonshi* (History of great Japan), although it was not completed until some fifteen years after his death. It was also Mitsukuni who actually requested the abolition of the custom of *junshi* (ritual suicide on the death of one's lord) to the shogunate. In literature, he preferred Japanese to Chinese, and vigorously supported the Shinto religion rather than Buddhism. His descendants were staunch supporters of imperial restoration and virulently anti-foreigner.

🔶 　 🔶 　 🔶

In educating a child, strong chastisement is not only unbeneficial, but in oppressing the light of his *ki*,[1] that ki may be obstructed. It is essential that the child be allowed to do as he will, but then led with understanding as the opportunity arises.

It is said that children in the fief were allowed to carry on freely and noisily in Mitsukuni's presence, but he never reprimanded them. The children then, at some point, were aware of their actions and improved their behavior.

---

1. *Ki* (Chinese, *ch'i*): the matter/energy that pervades the universe.

For the man who would be a warrior, death is not particularly difficult; it is the manner of dying that is difficult. It is not the way to live when you should not be living, or to die when you should not be dead.

"Books to Span the East and West"

Tuttle Publishing was founded in 1832 in the small New England town of Rutland, Vermont [USA]. Our core values remain as strong today as they were then—to publish best-in-class books which bring people together one page at a time. In 1948, we established a publishing outpost in Japan—and Tuttle is now a leader in publishing English-language books about the arts, languages and cultures of Asia. The world has become a much smaller place today and Asia's economic and cultural influence has grown. Yet the need for meaningful dialogue and information about this diverse region has never been greater. Over the past seven decades, Tuttle has published thousands of books on subjects ranging from martial arts and paper crafts to language learning and literature—and our talented authors, illustrators, designers and photographers have won many prestigious awards. We welcome you to explore the wealth of information available on Asia at **www.tuttlepublishing.com**.

Published by Tuttle Publishing, an imprint of Periplus Editions (HK) Ltd.

www.tuttlepublishing.com

Original Japanese work *Sengoku busho goroku* by Tadashi Kamiko, 1977.

English translation © William Scott Wilson 2023.

Pages 32–46, 98–102, 107–110, 114–117 were first translated in *The Pocket Samurai,* translated and edited by William Scott Wilson, © 2015 by William Scott Wilson. Reprinted by arrangement with Shambhala Publications, Inc., Boulder, CO. www.shambhala.com.

Library of Congress Control Number in process.

ISBN 978-4-8053-1741-9

TUTTLE PUBLISHING® is a registered trademark of Tuttle Publishing, a division of Periplus Editions (HK) Ltd.

Distributed by:

North America, Latin America & Europe
Tuttle Publishing
364 Innovation Drive
North Clarendon
VT 05759 9436, USA
Tel: 1(802) 773 8930
Fax: 1(802) 773 6993
info@tuttlepublishing.com
www.tuttlepublishing.com

Asia Pacific
Berkeley Books Pte Ltd
3 Kallang Sector #04-01
Singapore 349278
Tel: (65) 6741-2178
Fax: (65) 6741-2179
inquiries@periplus.com.sg
www.tuttlepublishing.com

Japan
Tuttle Publishing
Yaekari Building, 3rd Floor
5-4-12 Osaki Shinagawa-ku
Tokyo 141 0032 Japan
Tel: 81 (3) 5437 0171
Fax: 81 (3) 5437 0755
sales@tuttle.co.jp
www.tuttle.co.jp

26 25 24 23   5 4 3 2 1   2212CM

Printed in China